After you have read the research report, please give us your frank opinion on the contents. All comments—large or small, complimentary or caustic—will be appreciated. Mail them to CADRE/AR, Building 1400, 401 Chennault Circle, Maxwell AFB AL 36112-6428.

XIX Tactical Air Command and ULTRA

Shwedo

Patton's Force Enhancers in the 1944 Campaign in France

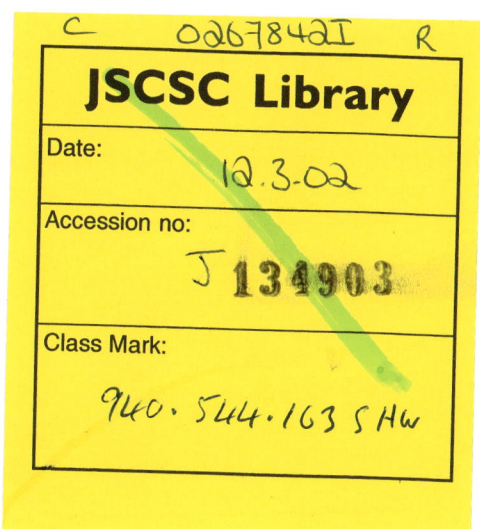

C   0267842I   R

JSCSC Library

Date: 12.3.02

Accession no: J134903

Class Mark: 940.544.163 SHW

Thank you for your assistance

Hobson Library

412325

COLLEGE OF AEROSPACE DOCTRINE, RESEARCH AND EDUCATION

AIR UNIVERSITY

XIX Tactical Air Command and ULTRA
Patton's Force Enhancers in the 1944 Campaign in France

BRADFORD J. "BJ" SHWEDO
Major, USAF

CADRE Paper No. 10

Air University Press
Maxwell Air Force Base, Alabama 36112-6615

May 2001

Library of Congress Cataloging-in-Publication Data

Shwedo, Bradford J., 1963–
    XIX Tactical Air Command and ULTRA : Patton's force enhancers in the 1944 campaign in France / Bradford J. Shwedo.
        p. cm. — (CADRE paper ; 10)
    At head of title: College of Aerospace Doctrine, Research, and Education, Air University.
    Includes bibliographical references.
    ISBN 1-58566-089-2
        1. World War, 1939–1945—Campaigns—France. 2. Patton, George S. (George Smith), 1885–1945. 3. ULTRA (Intelligence system) 4. World War, 1939–1945—Military intelligence—United States. 5. World War, 1939–1945— Cryptography. 6. United States. Army Air Forces. Tactical Air Command, 19th— History. 7. World War, 1939–1945—Regimental histories—United States. 8. Close air support. I. Title: 19 Tactical Air Command and Ultra. II. Title: Nineteen Tactical Air Command and Ultra. III. Title. IV. Series.

D761 .S49 2001
940.54′214—dc21   2001022416

Disclaimer

Opinions, conclusions, and recommendations expressed or implied within are solely those of the author and do not necessarily represent the views of Air University, the United States Air Force, the Department of Defense, or any other US government agency. Cleared for public release: distribution unlimited.

This CADRE Paper and others in the series are available electronically at the Air University Research Web site http://research.maxwell.af.mil under "Research Papers" then "Special Collections."

CADRE Papers

CADRE Papers are occasional publications sponsored by the Airpower Research Institute of Air University's College of Aerospace Doctrine, Research and Education (CADRE). Dedicated to promoting understanding of aerospace power theory and application, these studies are published by the Air University Press and broadly distributed to the US Air Force, the Department of Defense and other governmental organizations, leading scholars, selected institutions of higher learning, public policy institutes, and the media.

All military members and civilian employees assigned to Air University are invited to contribute unclassified manuscripts. Manuscripts should deal with air and/or space power history, theory, doctrine or strategy, or with joint or combined service matters bearing on the application of air and/or space power.

Authors should submit three copies of a double-spaced, typed manuscript and an electronic version of the manuscript on a 3.5-inch disk(s) along with a brief (200-word maximum) abstract. The electronic file should be compatible with Microsoft Windows and Microsoft Word—Air University Press uses Word as its standard word-processing program.

Please send inquiries or comments to:
Dean of Research
Airpower Research Institute
CADRE
401 Chennault Circle
Maxwell AFB AL 36112-6428
Tel: (334) 953-6875
DSN 493-6875
Fax: (334) 953-6739
Internet: james.titus@maxwell.af.mil

Contents

Maps

Photographs

Foreword

Gen George S. Patton Jr. remains one of the most storied commanders of World War II. Patton's spectacularly successful drive across France in August–September 1944 as commander of the US Third Army was perhaps his greatest campaign.

Many biographers have attributed Patton's achievements almost exclusively to his masterful employment of armor and to an innate sixth sense that enabled him to anticipate the moves of his opponents. Drawing heavily on declassified ULTRA intelligence reports, the records of XIX Tactical Air Command, and postwar interrogations of German commanders, Maj Bradford J. Shwedo's *XIX Tactical Air Command and ULTRA: Patton's Force Enhancers in the 1944 Campaign in France* sheds new light on Patton's generalship and suggests that Patton's penchant for risk and audacity may have been less the product of a sixth sense than of his confidence in ULTRA and tactical airpower. Timely and highly accurate ULTRA intelligence afforded Patton knowledge of German capabilities and enabled him to shape his operations to exploit mounting German weakness. Airpower provided top cover, punched through German concentrations, guarded Patton's right flank, and furnished crucial airlift support while disrupting enemy lines of communication.

Whatever Patton's personal intuitive gifts, he deserves full marks for skillfully integrating the ground scheme of maneuver, airpower, and intelligence into the overall strategy of the Third Army. Major Shwedo shows in some detail how Patton used both ULTRA and conventional operational intelligence to identify German vulnerabilities and then coordinated ground maneuver forces and airpower to exploit those vulnerabilities and create new ones. The synergy between courageous leadership and airpower, highly mobile ground forces, and superb intelligence—each creating opportunities for the other—took the Third Army and XIX TAC from Normandy to within 50 miles of the German border in less than 45 days.

General Patton's masterful employment of armor, airpower, and intelligence in a campaign fought more than 50 years ago is a textbook example of the sophisticated fusion of airpower, ground power, and information in the planning and execution of a fast-moving military operation. It is also a case study in flexibility, innovation, and boldness at the operational level of war. For all those reasons, Patton's campaign in France merits the attention of latter-day air and ground warriors who must meet the security challenges of the twenty-first century.

Originally written as a master's thesis for Air University's School of Advanced Airpower Studies (SAAS), *XIX Tactical Air Command and ULTRA* was selected by the Air Force Historical Foundation as the best SAAS thesis for academic year 1999–2000. The College of Aerospace Doctrine, Research and Education is pleased to make this excellent study available to the US Air Force and beyond.

JAMES R. W. TITUS
Dean of Research
Air University

About the Author

Maj Bradford J. "BJ" Shwedo is an intelligence officer who has served in various assignments within the intelligence community. Currently, he is assigned to the Joint Staff at the Pentagon as an operations officer in the Directorate of Operations, Information Operations (J-39). His unit level experience was with the 53d Fighter Squadron during Operations Desert Shield and Desert Storm, and he commanded a signals intelligence site in Korea. Staff positions include assignments as intelligence support officer to new weapons acquisitions and as chief of Offensive Information Warfare on the Air Staff. Major Shwedo is a graduate of the US Air Force Academy, Defense Intelligence College, Air Command and Staff College, and the School of Advanced Airpower Studies. He and his wife Alison have one son, Mac.

Acknowledgments

Much of this study is based on extensive primary source research. Some reside in archives; and to the novice, archives usually necessitate enormous amounts of support from experts. This study was no exception to that rule. Specifically, I thank The Citadel archives employees for providing Lt Col Melvin C. Helfers's personal papers and three videotaped interviews; these greatly aided this project. I also recognize Joe Caver and his associates at the Air Force Historical Research Agency for providing unlimited access to Gen O. P. Weyland's collection and the unit reports from XIX Tactical Air Command (TAC). The Auburn University Library afforded me unlimited access to the ULTRA messages used in this work, which allowed the prolonged activity of associating specific ULTRA messages with orders, authors' accounts, and troop movements. Invaluable background information was provided through two outstanding Americans, Andy Anderson and Frederick Vosburg, both of whom were intelligence experts at the XIX TAC. I express my respect and gratitude to my thesis advisor, Dr. Harold R. Winton. He offered encouragement, direction, and advice on all aspects of this paper. Dr. Winton's sense of humor and tenacity pushed this document through numerous revisions. My reader, Col Stephen D. Chiabotti, had similar attributes; and his inputs significantly aided my paper. I thank my wife Alison and our son Mac for their support and all the fun times along the way. While I owe so much to many others, any errors in interpretation or expression of the facts are mine alone. Therefore, any errors lie solely with the author.

Chapter 1

Introduction

The superior efficiency and cooperation afforded to this Army by the forces under your command is the best example of the combined use of air and ground troops I have ever witnessed.

—George S. Patton Jr.
(letter to the commander,
XIX TAC, August 1944)

General Patton's use of ULTRA in his historic drive across France is a fitting thesis for a tactical epic . . . One message, as at Avranches, may turn the spear points of a German Army and save an entire campaign from disaster. Each day brings some item of value and interest and in many cases, the item is the motive force behind whole divisions. The service is so incredibly valuable that it requires time for an intelligent person to believe that it is really reliable. The first impression by other than the gullible is that it is too good to be true.

—Maj Warrack Wallace, 18 September 1944
Bletchley Park Observer to US Third Army

In the course of military history, few generals have risen to the achievements of Gen George S. Patton Jr. and his Third US Army (USA). One of General Patton's most significant accomplishments was his historic drive across France in 1944. Attacking in three different directions (westward—Brittany, south—Loire River, east—Paris to the Moselle River), the Third Army moved farther and faster than any other army in the history of warfare.[1] At one point during this campaign, Third Army advanced along a 90-mile front that ran along the Loire River, which gave Patton a combined flank and front of 450 miles.[2] During this month-and-a-half offensive, the Third

Army liberated 41,000 square miles of enemy territory in its drive from Normandy to within 50 miles of the German border.[3] Patton's exploitation of the situation in the August and September 1944 scenario became "the beginning of the end" for Germany. Most importantly, his rapid drives permitted astonishing gains at relatively low losses (approximate totals of German losses were 32,000 killed; 96,500 wounded; and 94,199 taken as prisoners of war [POW]; United States [US] losses were 4,575 killed; 23,794 wounded; and 6,156 missing).[4] The extraordinary results of this campaign have led many historians to wonder what was the secret behind Patton's success.

Most of the studies associated with Patton focus on the glorious deeds, bravery, and tenacity of the Third Army. This narrow perspective may not thoroughly explain the details behind Patton's success. His unorthodox schemes remain the focus of debate concerning the genius of Patton. Unfortunately, due to Patton's premature death in 1945 and the limited information available to researchers immediately after the war, many post–World War II histories fostered a myriad of myths that persist to this day. These histories run the gamut. Some credit Patton's success to mythical qualities and claim he had "a sixth sense—which enabled him to foresee situations that were developing and make dispositions to meet them."[5] Others attack his strategies in France for his perceived blatant disregard for flank protection. One author said the way that Patton fixed his logistic problems "does not bear examination, in terms of how a responsible senior commander should behave."[6] Another author characterized Patton's drive across France as a "reckless exploitation" of the situation.[7] Contrary to these accounts, Patton was not guided by a sixth sense or reckless action; and contemporary commanders, through careful examination, can extract many lessons from the campaign fought in France a half century ago.

During this drive Patton rapidly exploited a fluid front as his area of responsibility (AOR) grew exponentially. The manner in which Patton exploited the battlefields in France has often provoked controversy. However, he provided some clues to his success when in late August he stated, "to attack with the limited forces I have now available—since I occupy a 300 mile front [and had lost the XV Corps to Hodges]—I am taking chances, but I am convinced that the situation in the German Army warrants the taking of such risks."[8] In this case Patton knew he had to capitalize on the window of opportunity that was present in the summer of 1944. But as his AOR increased and his manpower strengths remained constant, he also realized he had to devise economy-of-force measures. He accomplished this task through various force-enhancing schemes that entailed some unorthodox employment of his units. Although these unorthodox schemes remain the focus of debate concerning the genius of Patton, recently declassified sources afford insight into some of Patton's actions and the calculations and estimates upon which these actions were based.

Immediately after declassification of ULTRA intelligence records,* Gen Ira C. Eaker, commander of the Eighth and Fifteenth Air Forces, stated that "virtually all of the historical accounts of the great battles of World War II must now be reexamined in the light of ULTRA's extraordinary disclosures."[9] Unfortunately, most of the senior leadership of World War II did not live long enough to cite the benefits of ULTRA, but one who did provide an idea of the advantages it could afford a commander. In 1975 when Gen Elwood R. Quesada, commander of XI Tactical Air Command (TAC), was asked the value of ULTRA messages, he said,

> They were particularly valuable. They would tell us where certain units were. They would tell us where they might be going. They would tell us in one way or the other what the state of their alert was. They would often tell us what the effect of certain actions of ours was on them. It would often do that. That was a common source of information, which of course, would often make us grin. Sometimes be embarrassed too, I might add. And so, this information was not only to inform us what was happening at the time, but would confirm the effect of our action on prior days and prior weeks. It wasn't uncommon for us to get a verbatim copy of a message through the ULTRA system that was sent to

---

*Coined by the British, ULTRA was the code name for high-grade signals intelligence derived from German secret radio communications. Such enemy messages were known as Enigma communications, after the sophisticated German cipher machine used to encrypt them. By 1940 the British were routinely intercepting, deciphering, translating, and analyzing a large portion of German Enigma traffic. The resulting ULTRA intelligence gave the British, and later the Americans, extraordinarily accurate information on the capabilities, vulnerabilities, and intentions of their German opponents. ULTRA remained a secret for almost 30 years after the war. Its existence was first revealed in 1974 when retired RAF Group Capt Frederick W. Winterbotham published *The Ultra Secret*.

the German field commanders, Army group commanders as an example, and from Hitler and his entourage, and we would often get the message before the field commander got it. And you could tell that by the field commander's response "I got your message yesterday afternoon," but we would have had it yesterday morning. That happened time and time again. It was a very helpful thing.[10]

Because of the beneficial possibilities cited by Generals Quesada and Eaker's assertion which insists that the great battles must be reexamined in the light of ULTRA, it may now be possible to fathom the role of this special intelligence in General Patton's success.

Another area often neglected by historians during discussions concerning Patton is his use of airpower. Patton made every effort to emphasize the contributions of airpower during this campaign; and he often started press conferences by stating, "Now I would appreciate it if you all could integrate in your stories the Third Army and the XIX Tactical Air Command, because the XIX TAC has done a great job with us."[11] Gen Carl A. Spaatz confirmed the great job done by the XIX TAC with the Third Army. After the drive across France, General Spaatz noted, "What you've seen is the greatest example of air-ground cooperation that has ever been or will ever be."[12] Like accounts of ULTRA, many of the airpower stories that motivated Patton and Spaatz's praise are untold—still buried in the archives. Although Patton's ground scheme of maneuver has been well documented, its relationship to the force enhancers represented by ULTRA and airpower has yet to be examined in detail.

This study examines the relationship among ULTRA, Patton's ground scheme of maneuver, and the operations of XIX TAC. Patton did not live long enough to reveal the impact of ULTRA intelligence on his battle plans, but declassification efforts have shed a new light on this topic. Archival material provides a useful basis for assessment of airpower's contributions and an expanded view of history.

To better understand the relationship among Patton's force enhancers, this study examines ULTRA reports and compares them to the standard accounts of the various battles. After-action reports by the ULTRA officers at Third Army and XIX TAC headquarters serve as a foundation. Recollections are evaluated against secondary historical accounts to better ensure accuracy and become the starting point for associating and tracing individual messages to operational decisions. These ULTRA reports are compared to memoirs and diaries to identify suggestive but understandably guarded references by senior decision makers. All of this information discloses how Patton took advantage of the fluid environment of 1944. Patton's effective and sometimes unorthodox employment of airpower and ULTRA allowed him to take risks and dictate situations that made him and his troops the most successful and feared forces in the European theater.

This study traces Patton's higher tactical and operational decisions from the hedgerows of Normandy in early August 1944 to the banks of the Moselle River, just 50 miles from the German border. During this campaign Patton devised unique systems to exploit the reciprocal and force-enhancing capabilities of ULTRA, airpower, and ground scheme of maneuver. The examination of the relationships among these three tools in the operational artist's kit bag serves several functions. First, it allows us to understand more fully the reasons behind Third US Army's rapid and successful drive across France. Second, it provides insight into the process by which a practitioner of the operational art makes the fine judgments between opportunity and risk and employs all the principal tools at his disposal to exploit the former and mitigate the latter. Third, it suggests how these same tools could be usefully combined in the technologically enhanced era of the twenty-first century.

Notes

1. George Forty, *Patton's Third Army at War* (London: Arms and Armour Press, 1990), 10.

2. Oscar W. Koch and Robert G. Hays, *G-2: Intelligence for Patton* (Philadelphia: Whitmore Publishing, 1971), 66.

3. Brenton G. Wallace, *Patton and His Third Army* (Washington, D.C.: Military Service Publishing Co., 1946), 88.

4. Robert S. Allen, *Lucky Forward* (New York: Vanguard Press, 1947), 144.

5. Fred Ayer Jr., *Before the Colors Fade* (Boston: Houghton Mifflin, 1964), iii.

6. Ronald Lewin, *Montgomery as Military Commander* (Conshohocken, Pa.: Combined Publishing, 1998), 232.

7. Martin Blumenson, *The Patton Papers*, vol. 2, *1940–1945* (Boston: Houghton Mifflin, 1974), 528.

8. Ibid.

9. Ira C. Eaker, Microfilm 23342—Personal Collection of I. C. Eaker—"ULTRA Goes to War" (Air Force Historical Research Center: Eaker Collection, 29 December 1974), 1.

10. Ralph Stephenson, Report K239.0512-838—"Interview with Lt Gen Elwood R. Quesada—ULTRA Section" (Air Force Historical Research Center: Quesada Collection, 13 May 1975), 7.

11. Blumenson, 539.

12. Frederick Vosburg, XIX TAC senior intelligence officer, telephone interview with the author, 24 March 2000.

Chapter 2

Key Players

I would like to learn from you something. I don't understand how you could more or less be everywhere at once. It seemed that if something was hit in the rear areas, interdictions and so on, supply establishments, reserve German troops moving somewhere, you would show up and clobber them. But then when your army was going to attack or defend—either one, but usually attacking—you had all kinds of airplanes helping them. How could you be everywhere all the time?

—*Generalfeldmarschall* Gerd von Rundstedt
(Question asked of the XIX TAC
commander during an interrogation)

During and after the war, Germans on the western front, at all levels of command, consistently pointed to Allied airpower as one of the main factors contributing to their defeat. *Generalfeldmarschall* Gerd von Rundstedt provided numerous examples of how Allied air operations ruined many of his battle plans throughout the European campaign. By mid-1944 the balance for air superiority began to tip in the favor of the Allies. When von Rundstedt was asked during interrogations after World War II what would have been different if the air force elements had been at parity prior to D day, he flatly stated "The invasion would have never succeeded."[1] Von Rundstedt further highlighted the force-enhancing effects of airpower when he said, "These attacks were painful for moving our troops, our supplies and our gas. The tactical attacks in France on railroad communications were devastating, all the more so as they were repeated like clockwork again and again immediately after we repaired the damage. On the roads our convoys or a single M/T [motor transport] could not move during the day. We could never count on when a certain division would arrive at its destination."[2] Von Rundstedt's respect for Allied airpower was no different before he became a POW. He stated in a message sent to higher headquarters during the war that "Allied air attacks to block railway transports to battle areas were very large in scale and had corresponding effect . . . Allies exactly informed on German bringing up of forces by recce and considerable activity by agents."[3] Von Rundstedt did not live long enough to find out that agents and reconnaissance were not the only things that were informing the Allies. More important was the Allies' ability to rapidly apply airpower against these targets. This, along with their new advantage in air superiority, was the product of years of experience in North Africa and Italy.

Evolution of Airpower

One of the lessons from North Africa and Italy was the need for improved air-ground cooperation. Therefore, it was agreed prior to the Normandy invasion that air and ground commanders would live in the same quarters, use the same operations center, and—most importantly—would "coordinate and not subordinate" operations as "coequals."[4] These decisions eventually were spelled out in Field Manual (FM) 100-20, *Command and Employment of Air Power.* While some air commanders used FM 100-20 to convince their ground compatriots that they were on coequal status, XIX TAC took it as a starting point to evolve doctrine to fit the situation that existed in 1944 France. General Patton described this evolution which became the basis for the Third Army's XIX TAC's air-ground team:

> We have seen the attempts of air and ground to work together for years but it was only on the 1st of August [1944] that it really worked. First, air was subservient to the ground forces. That was wrong. Then air and ground were set as things apart and that was wrong for it was quite evident that we were not getting along. When, in those days, we would ask for support from air the request might be made at 8:30 in the morning and planes in inadequate numbers would arrive at perhaps 1:30 in the afternoon. I do not say this in criticism but I wish to point out the lack of understanding of the system of getting them there.[5]

Patton's people knew the system was broken and made changes that may have appeared to be unorthodox, but these schemes significantly exploited the opportunities that existed in August 1944. FM 100-20 directed a list of prioritized tactical airpower missions and proposed the highest priority missions for tactical air forces were air superiority, interdiction, and, last, close air support (CAS) because it was "the most difficult to control, most expensive, and are in general, least effective."[6] XIX TAC took a different approach. They emphasized CAS and interdiction (42 percent and 40 percent of sorties, respectively) while their sister, IX TAC, had more conventional employment methods (27 percent CAS and 46 percent interdiction).[7]

The situation in Europe dictated that CAS should become a higher priority, but this concept strayed from the teachings of that time. The Army Air Force School of Applied Tactics claimed before the D-day invasion: "It is almost impossible to employ third phase operations [CAS] where bomb lines cannot be maintained. This phase depends for success upon teamwork and cooperation. It is best employed on a stable front, where preplanned attacks can soften up the enemy for a breakthrough by ground forces."[8] Again, General Patton's forces took a different approach. To ensure the best possible CAS and interdiction sorties for his rapidly moving forces, Patton recommended that bomb lines be abolished and that fighter-bombers be allowed to attack freely against any clearly recognizable targets of opportunity.[9] The Army Air Force School of Applied Tactics was correct in determining that CAS was dependent upon teamwork and cooperation, which became another area where Patton employed unique solutions to ensure success.

XIX TAC found the Army Air Corps manning for air liaison officers (ALO) to be inadequate to support air-ground operations. They improvised manning and equipment that expanded their ALO organization by a factor of three over the amount allowed by Air Corps tables of organization.[10] The coordination among all elements was focused on shortening the decision cycle for air attacks. XIX TAC found existing warning and intelligence functions disjointed and unsatisfactory, and they described their solution with the following comment: "To overcome this, all aircraft warning units, fighter control squadrons, and radio intercept 'Y' service [intelligence] have been organized into a provisional Tactical Control Group and placed directly under the control of the Advanced Headquarters, XIX Tactical Air Command."[11] The evolution of this improvised system led Patton to say "formerly, . . . we could never talk to each other but now we can curse the living daylights out of each other!"[12] While Patton points out one of the added benefits of this organization, the results on the battlefield truly displayed the merits of his system.

General Patton and his forces believed the summer of 1944 offered a window of opportunity to end the war quickly, but this plan rested on the assumption that Third Army could exploit the fluid situation by rapid drives through the *Wehrmacht.* All actions sought to increase the pace of the advance. Gen O. P. Weyland, the XIX TAC's commander, best described the sometimes unconventional nature of the drives across France with the following account:

> Well, the Germans were fairly discombobulated. We, of course, endeavored to keep him in that shape and that was part of the interdiction program. To see that they couldn't move their reserves. Or if they did, to get them mixed up and whatnot. So they'd run these armored columns into the Germans, and I'd violate what used to be an old principle of tactical air power "Don't use air power against something that the artillery can hit." Well, time was of the essence. So I said to he-- with that. Here, they were moving, so by the time they'd stop a column and deploy their artillery and whatnot . . . He--, it might take them an hour or two. I'd have fighter-bombers out in front and we'd try to take care of anything out there. But sometimes there'd be concealed stuff. So then they'd yell. I'd have an Air Force liaison officer in the lead tank who communicated with the fighter group that was working up front somewhere . . . Whistle them back, and they'd be there in three minutes. Wham! Wham! Wham! They'd keep rolling.[13]

Patton had created a truly integrated air-ground team, and this feeling permeated the lowest echelons of command. Gen Paul Harkins (Patton's deputy chief of staff) fondly recalled this unique teamwork when he said, "The 19th TAC would fly in weather that was absolutely forbidden for anybody else to fly in. If a tank cut-out or got damaged out in front of the lines and the others couldn't move, the [19th] TAC would come in under cloud cover and go in and strafe around until somebody could go out and pull the tank out."[14] This support worked both ways. The 4th Armored Division diverted resources to secure a downed airman through a call from his squadron mates, and the XIX TAC repeatedly used Third Army artillery fire for flak suppression.[15] Patton fostered this relationship, which was significantly better than the air-ground cooperation in North Africa; and he took great pride in describing this new kinship. "Now the situation has cleared up wonderfully because the soldiers got to know each other and about the other fellow's organization. There is a steady stream of pilots going for visits to my units at the front to see how my ground soldiers live. And I also know that many of my own men are making it a practice of calling on the pilots to help drain bottles of captured enemy merchandise. And this spirit of comradeship is helping out in many ways."[16] This comradeship may have flourished at the bottom, but it clearly had its roots at the top.

General Patton's planning for the European campaign began in England, and he wasted no time finding a commander for his air arm. General Weyland recalled harboring some anxiety about his new command. But early in the job, the spirit of 1943 Casablanca agreements overcame many of his concerns as related in the following story.

> Initially, this was not looked upon as a highly desirable assignment. General Patton had a reputation as being hard to work with, and he had a rather low regard for air power. However, this was to change rapidly . . . Whereas many ground commanders still believed that tactical air power should be subordinated to the ground force commander, General Patton agreed with me that he would command the ground and that I would run the associated tactical air forces. At the same time we both laid our cards on the table. We planned and executed our respective responsibilities in the closest of coordination . . . From an early attitude of skepticism, General Patton went to the other extreme. He thought the XIX Tactical Air Command could do no wrong.[17]

Considering General Weyland's background, it is not surprising that the two generals got along so well. Weyland had spent most of his Air Corps career in tactical aircraft and had served several tours directly attached to ground units. This provided him added credibility because as he pointed out, to the average Air Corps officer, "ground organization tactics were pretty much of a mystery to them—it was not to me."[18] Patton demanded competence and results, and it did not take long for Weyland to display both. Early in the campaign, Patton was impressed with roadways filled with dead Germans and destroyed equipment all credited to the XIX TAC; and this time it was Patton asking Weyland to drain a bottle of bourbon for his efforts. Weyland later admitted, "Well, we killed that bottle of bourbon, I think. And from a degree of mutual respect, this brightened up into a very close and lasting friendship."[19]

Generals George S. Patton Jr. and O. P. Weyland

Understanding ULTRA

ULTRA was another area where Patton used his experience in North Africa and Italy to improve both relationships and performance. Although Patton disliked many of the British representatives associated with the ULTRA system, he knew this source of intelligence was far too important to waste due to his prejudices. Patton knew that with every dutiful message the Germans sent, they were compromising another aspect of their operations. This was true because early in the war, the Allies had broken the Germans' highest level of communications; and Patton, as Group Capt F. W. Winterbotham—senior RAF representative at Bletchley Park—later noted, "never failed to use every opportunity that ULTRA gave him to bust open the enemy."[20]

These opportunities were afforded because much of the German message traffic was transmitted via wireless sets employing a cryptological machine called Enigma. The breaking of this machine's codes began in the interwar years through a multinational effort. The Poles initiated the process in 1929; and the French aided in this effort in 1932 by presenting to the British German army Enigma intercepts, a commercial Enigma machine (originally designed in 1919 to protect business secrets), and two Enigma manuals.[21] The German military made numerous improvements on the original, which made the number of possible cipher combinations (or keys) "500 million million million . . . million [the word million being written a total of 15 times]."[22] In 1939, with World War II on the horizon, the Poles shared all of their knowledge with the French and the British; but within one year, the British were fighting the Enigma battle alone.

Although the Germans on occasion questioned the security of their wireless communications, they placed their confidence in the above calculations; and that misplaced confidence became a significant factor in their defeat in World War II. The British launched an all-out attack on the Enigma machine and its codes. This effort had top priority for all resources, and it rapidly expanded to an organization of 10,000 people who had an almost limitless budget. It was a complex program. The system required a large signals intelligence (SIGINT) intercept infrastructure, which would relay raw intercepts to the code breakers located 50 miles north of London at Bletchley Park.[23] At Bletchley Park, the code breakers used early computers called Bombas to help break the codes; and then the messages were translated, analyzed, and prioritized.[24] The British quickly discovered the tactical applicability of this information and built up an infrastructure to facilitate this process. They established special liaison units (SLU) that were colocated with operational forces to push this information down to army command level. This secret information was held at the highest levels and was classified Top Secret ULTRA. The ULTRA recipient list was kept to the bare minimum; but when the United States entered the war, the circle expanded.

Patton's first introduction to ULTRA was in 1942 during Operation Torch in North Africa. During this period it was the British SLU's responsibility to provide ULTRA information to the commands. However, in late 1943 it was agreed that each country "would disseminate ULTRA to its own commands."[25] This decision was one of the significant factors that made ULTRA so effective in France. Prior to this agreement, the British SLUs were Bletchley Park's only representatives to the field commands; and they were not good salesmen at Patton's headquarters. They had no intention of becoming team players and constantly reminded people through their actions that they did not fall under Patton's command.

The first step towards changing Patton's mind about ULTRA involved finding a new salesman. The success of the 1943 ULTRA agreement became apparent when Patton met his first American ULTRA officer. He enthusiastically asked his G-2, "Why haven't I been informed about this Major at Third Army Headquarters?"[26] His G-2 replied, "Since we had such a bad experience with British intelligence and signal troops (SLU) attached in Africa and Sicily, I felt it best not to mention their presence and mission to you."[27] The employment of a competent team player transformed ULTRA from a daily one-page synopsis in North Africa and Sicily to an extravagant daily briefing and a 24-hour access to the commanders of Third Army and XIX TAC in France.

The above access was unique to the American commands, and that may be due to the extraordinary ULTRA personnel under General Patton's command. Outside of Patton's Third Army, the US ULTRA program was largely an incestuous organization whose senior leader was a civilian lawyer named Alfred McCormack. McCormack largely focused on barristers to fill the ULTRA ranks because he believed "that lawyers as a class are better fitted for intelligence work."[28] Author Thomas Parrish noted that this practice left the program with numerous inexperienced personnel, of which "a surprising proportion [consisted] of Alfred McCormack's fellow Princeton Tigers."[29] Parrish made an additional observation about this ULTRA corps. "These ULTRA officers would be young men of low rank, almost all of them civilians at heart, and relatively new to the army. But generals must not, for such reasons, brush them off. What these men would have that was possessed by no one else in any of the commands, was training . . . in the handling of items of signal intelligence."[30] The Third Army ULTRA officer called this training a British joke where "the main item of equipment used was a mug for drinking tea, the dirtier the better"; and he claimed, "I don't remember learning anything important."[31] This may have been true because the Third Army ULTRA officer was not new to the Army, which is probably why generals did not brush him off.

Civilians at heart—relatively new to the army—were recipes for disaster at Third Army headquarters; and someone had the foresight to send a unique ULTRA officer to Patton's staff, Lt Col Melvin C. Helfers. In direct contrast to lawyer McCormack's philosophy, a firm credo in Third Army's G-2 organization was that "intelligence officers are made, not born."[32] While the other commands were struggling with their on-the-job trainees, Colonel Helfers was ready to perform his duties. Helfers was a 1937 Citadel graduate, and he was the only Regular Army officer selected for ULTRA duties.[33] He knew what was important; and, unlike his contemporaries, he had the immediate confidence of his commanders, which helped him fuse his information into Third Army operations. Helfers held little regard for his higher headquarters counterparts, and he described the Twelfth US Army Group G-2 section as "overrun with a bunch of civilian lawyer flunkies."[34] Unlike his higher headquarters, Helfers had an excellent working relationship with his Army Air Forces ULTRA compatriot.

Maj Harry M. Grove was the ULTRA officer assigned to the XIX TAC, and he too broke the stereotype of the typical American ULTRA officer. Major Grove also had an operational background and called himself an "Air Force retread."[35] Grove had been a pilot in World War I; and when he was recalled to duty during World War II, he had instant credibility. He and Helfers also carried on the air-ground cooperation within ULTRA channels. Early in the campaign, Grove received "a request from Gen Patton's Chief of Staff through Lt Col Melvin Helfers . . . that a verbal presentation of ULTRA information on the

GAF [German Air Force] be given to Gen Patton and his staff at the regular ULTRA briefing."[36] This briefing was the main conduit for incorporation of ULTRA into Third Army operations. Patton had two staff meetings each morning—a large formalized briefing that was preceded by the much smaller ULTRA briefing. Major Grove recalled these meetings as follows,

Lt Col (then major) Melvin C. Helfers's ULTRA Briefing to Patton

> It was the custom of Gen Weyland and Col Browne to attend the regular morning ULTRA briefing of Gen Patton and his Staff . . . It should be stated here both generals and staffs were extremely attentive listeners, and gave the most serious consideration to ULTRA information. This interest was indicated by the concentration of attention during the briefing, as it was the rule to ask no questions during the verbal presentation, but afterward, many intelligent questions were asked and opinions requested based on the material at hand. It afforded the writer the greatest satisfaction to observe the influence of source information on the conduct of operations.[37]

Helfers reflected upon these little meetings by stating, "General Patton must have considered this small group his privy counsel, and he did not hesitate to let his thoughts wander with them and to discuss future operations with them."[38] Col Oscar W. Koch, Patton's G-2, had similar memories of these sessions. In his guarded 1970 account, he observed that the "presentation would be followed by a period of thinking out loud by all present . . . If the enemy does so and so, General Patton would ask, what do you think of our doing this?"[39] ULTRA started the day for the Third Army and XIX TAC, but that was not this information's only outlet. Both commanders also gave their ULTRA officers clearance to provide updates any time during the day that they deemed appropriate. General Weyland made this clear to Grove by stating that "he wanted to be awakened at once for any information that he could do something about, and it was left to the writer's (Grove) judgment and experience."[40] Within Patton's organization the ULTRA staff's judgment and experience were never in question.

The last aspects that helped to ensure success for Patton were his appreciation for intelligence and for his G-2. As a senior officer, Patton's understanding and enthusiasm for intelligence was even more unique than his serious support for co-equal status for airpower or for well-prepared ULTRA officers. He appreciated the opportunities ULTRA provided because unlike most field commanders, he had two tours as an intelligence officer (1925–28 and 1935–37).[41] Gen Omar Bradley best encapsulated the American view of an intelligence assignment when he reflected, "Misfits frequently found themselves assigned to intelligence duties. And in some stations G-2 became a dumping ground for officers ill-suited for command. I recall how scrupulously I avoided the branding that came with an intelligence assignment in my own career."[42] This practice led many senior commanders during the interwar years to grow indifferent when filling the various "2" positions on their staffs. This policy may be fine in peace, but it is disastrous in war. So while Patton was employing outstanding officers that were of the same caliber as General Weyland, other generals were filling their intelligence staffs apathetically with misfits and "officers ill-suited for command."

On top of Patton's intelligence apparatus as Third Army G-2 was Colonel Koch. He was an old friend of General Patton's from the Army Cavalry School, and he had followed Patton through his previous campaigns. Patton respected Koch; and he often praised Koch's efforts, once stating "I ought to know

Photo courtesy of US Army

Col Oscar W. Koch, Third Army's G-2

17

what I'm doing, I've got the best da--ed intelligence officer in any United States command."[43] When it came to ULTRA, Koch showed a maturity that other G-2s did not always possess. Appreciation for ULTRA ran the gamut among the various 2s. Some intelligence directors failed to see the value of this information, and the frustration of their subordinate staff was sometimes apparent: "It was difficult to properly present the 'source' [ULTRA] to the Commanding General and his deputies. This difficulty arose primarily because of the complete failure of the then A-2 to appreciate the value of the 'source' and the possibilities of its operational use. Fortunately, this A-2's services came to a speedy termination through the excellent marksmanship of a Wehrmacht submachine gunner."[44] On the opposite end of the scale, some G-2s totally embraced ULTRA. These officers were so infatuated by this source that they disregarded their duties as G-2s and became full-time ULTRA officers. As one ULTRA officer noted, that left him without a job and their associated armies without a G-2:

> Initially, the G-2 presented the signals, unsorted, unedited, and without comment, to the CG [commanding general] and C/S [chief of staff] twice daily. Later I was permitted to see them after everyone else. By keeping records and by plotting a map, I was able to show the G-2 that a good deal of valuable information was being overlooked. Gradually I was allowed first to sort and then to edit and by the beginning of the Ardennes offensive, the material was assembled and written up twice daily . . . then read to the CG by the G-2 . . . No briefing was ever done directly by the ULTRA representative.[45]

ULTRA was very enticing. Messages often provided everything a G-2 would want. German unit reports gave the exact order of battle strengths, locations, and conditions of morale. Logistic messages supplied the Allies with an interdiction playbook. Attack and movement orders gave the G-2 the ever-elusive intentions of the enemy, and damage or repair reports provided accurate bomb damage assessments and precise dates for follow-on strikes of repaired facilities. Some G-2s saw this as the answer to their dreams, but Koch took a different approach.

Accounts of ULTRA's contributions often ignore the potential pitfalls associated with its use. Some of these hazards were revealed in a May 1945 report: "The raw intercepted messages themselves never give a complete or sequential chronicle; the gaps must be filled by the knowledge of the inner administrative and operational procedures of the German armed forces and by deduction based on his knowledge. Often, ULTRA itself has been dangerously misleading. The ULTRA technique may decipher the message ordering an intended operation, but fail often to intercept the message that cancels or alters it."[46]

In contrast to many G-2s, Patton's director of intelligence took a balanced approach to exploiting ULTRA intelligence. Koch knew tracking the problems associated with ULTRA was a full-time job, which is why Helfers was the only ULTRA officer "in all the US armies who daily briefed the Army commander directly."[47] Koch knew his job was to provide the larger intelligence picture. ULTRA was just one facet of that greater picture, and Koch refused to let his other intelligence sections atrophy due to excessive reliance on this single source. Koch ensured all sections continued their work in spite of this intelligence windfall; and as one observer noted, this practice sometimes appeared to have redundant results:

> The regular G-2 sections, by dint of painstaking and intelligent piecing together of scraps gleaned from PW's (prisoners of war), captured documents and other sources, identified one morning at the regular meeting five enemy divisions in the line opposing the Third Army. This was good G-2 work. Yet, after the special briefing followed the regular briefing, Colonel Koch called to General Patton's attention that these five divisions had been identified by the recipients and placed on the ULTRA map as follows: two divisions a week before, two divisions three days before and one the preceding day. It was a common occurrence at the regular meeting for a G-2 man to identify a German division which had been spotted days before by ULTRA and had been announced at the special briefing. On two occasions the regular G-2 staff placed German divisions in the line which were actually in Italy, according to the last ULTRA report. At the special briefings following these occasions, it was stated that there had been no ULTRA message showing a movement from Italy. In each case, the divisions remained in Italy and the G-2 section, a week or so thereafter, corrected the mistakes which were due to PW's who strayed to France from their former units in Italy.[48]

Koch received numerous suggestions to indoctrinate (grant access to ULTRA intelligence) his order-of-battle team in order to eliminate the perceived redundancy of tasks and avoid any possible confusion due to the conflicting information presented by conventional sources of intelligence. Koch believed that this was inadvisable, and he stressed the need to create orders of battle "compiled exclusively from open sources."[49] This directive would pay handsome dividends in the prelude to the Battle of the Bulge and would also provide exceptional cover stories for the operational employment of ULTRA.

New Kid on the Block

Although Patton and Koch were veterans of North Africa and Sicily, before 1 January 1944 Third Army had been a training unit and would require some time to get ready for combat. The main body of Third Army arrived in England in March 1944, and preparations for tasks on the continent began immediately. Patton created an organization that was built for speed. Helfers's first impression "of Third Army Headquarters was that of an old-fashioned cavalry troop with General Patton as the troop commander and his four G's as his platoon commanders."[50] In order to ensure cavalry speed, Third Army was one of the first commands to use the war-room concept, not only in headquarters planning but also in the field of combat.[51] One of the first directives received by this war room was indicative of the coming campaign: "Third US Army Plan is indefinite since its deployment depends upon the situation at that time."[52] The vagueness was due to the fact that for the Normandy invasion, Third Army was considered a follow-on force not scheduled to be committed until D+28–D+30. The original Overlord plans had Third Army largely focused on Brittany; but soon after the commencement of operations, its aims would greatly expand.[53]

Third Army officially initiated operations on 1 August 1944 and found a situation that was perfect for Patton's style of warfare. The enemy troops opposing Third Army were not ready for Patton's rapid exploitation of the battlefield. The Seventh German Army opposite Patton's forces was battered by the previous months' operations. These German forces had become accustomed to the set-piece battles of the hedgerows, and as one quote attributed to Gen George C. Marshall attests, the Germans were about to meet a new adversary: "Bradley will lead the invasion, but he is a limited objective general. When we get moving, Patton is the man with the drive and imagination to do dangerous things fast."[54] Bradley's limited objectives in June and July significantly wore down the German army; and when Operation Cobra blasted a hole in the brittle lines, Patton's mobile forces were matchless to exploit this breakthrough.

By 31 May 1944, Third Army had 253,000 men; but it took time to channel these forces through the narrow bridgehead in Normandy in the months of July and August. During the initial phase of this operation, Patton had five armored and six infantry divisions. To increase the tempo of the attack, Patton used these armored divisions as Third Army's lead elements, with the infantry being employed to reduce any bypassed strong points. In order to maneuver these forces quickly, Patton employed informal techniques to reduce the time associated with Third Army's decision cycle.

As reflected in the earlier ULTRA section, Patton's planning for Third Army's operations often occurred in an informal atmosphere. Contrary to his popular image, during these planning sessions Patton jettisoned his legendary gruff personality. According to Helfers, "my experience with him was like a college professor conducting a seminar, easy going and he had a sense of humor."[55] Operational planning started with intelligence; and as one author noted, this practice had obvious benefits. "Patton never made a move without first consulting G-2. In planning, G-2 always had the first say. The usual procedure at other Headquarters was to decide what to do and then, perhaps, ask G-2 what was out front. Patton always got his information first and then acted on the basis of it. That explains why Third Army was never surprised and why it always smashed through vulnerable sectors in the enemy's lines."[56] In order to facilitate the rapid application of this information, Patton created various organizations to quickly move data within his front. This meant that his war room was constantly busy; and as Third Army's after-action reports indicate, many of their inputs were taken through informal telephone calls (more formal confirmation orders came via hard copy later).[57]

Every component within Patton's organization was built to focus on the rapid and efficient application of military force. While Patton was building this organization, he had the advantage of monitoring the ongoing operations in France, which allowed him to prepare his troops intelligently for their upcoming tasks. Patton impatiently watched the Battle for Normandy and confined his critiques to his diary and his inner circle of friends, but his comments offered an excellent preview of plans for the upcoming operations: "Sometimes I get desperate over the future. Brad and Hodges are such nothings. Their virtue is that they get along by doing nothing. I could break through in three days if I commanded. They try to push all along the front and have power nowhere. All that is necessary now is to take more chances by leading them with armored divisions and covering their advances with air bursts. Such an attack would have to be made on a narrow sector, whereas at present we are trying to attack all along the line."[58] Third Army arrived on the European continent at a time tailor-made for a commander who could exploit the fluid conditions that existed in August 1944. Patton was such a commander, and a foreshadowing of upcoming events is evident in the comments of a Navy lieutenant who witnessed Third Army's debarkation. "And when you see General Patton . . . you get the same feeling as when you saw Babe Ruth striding up to the plate. Here's a big guy who's going to kick the he-- out of something."[59]

Notes

1. O. P. Weyland, Report 168.7104-95—"Weyland's Interrogation of von Rundstedt at Bad Kissingen" (Albert F. Simpson Historical Research Center: Weyland Collection, 2 July 1945), 6.

2. Ibid., 4–5.

3. James D. Fellers, SRH-023—"Reports by US Army ULTRA Representatives in the European Theater of Operations" (National Archives: Record Group 457, 7 June 1945), 35.

4. Laurence S. Kuter, "God---mit Georgie," *Air Force Magazine*, February 1973, 55.

5. O. P. Weyland, Report 168.7104-101—"Talks by General Patton and General Weyland at Press Conference" (Albert F. Simpson Historical Research Center: Weyland Collection, 16 December 1944), 3.

6. Field Manual 100-20, *Command and Employment of Air Power*, 12.

7. David N. Spires, "Air Power for Patton's Army: The XIX Tactical Air Command in the Second World War," draft paper, June 1994, Boulder, Colo., 266.

8. Wasson J. Wilson and Henry F. Fitzmaurice, Report 248.401-19—lecture, "Command and Employment of Airpower" (Air Force Historical Research Center, 10 January 1945), 5.

9. Russell F. Weigley, *Eisenhower's Lieutenants: The Campaign of France and Germany, 1944–1945* (Bloomington, Ind.: Indiana University Press, 1981), 242.

10. XIX TAC Staff, Report 168.7104-64—"Twelve Thousand Fighter-Bomber Sorties" (Albert F. Simpson Historical Research Center: Weyland Collection, 30 September 1944), 1.

11. Ibid.

12. Weyland, Report 168.7104-101, 4.

13. Ralph Stephenson, Report K239.0512-813—"Interview with General O. P. Weyland" (Air Force Historical Research Center: Weyland Collection, 19 November 1974), 77–78.

14. James Hasdorff, Report K239.0512-522—"Interview with Gen Paul D. Harkins" (Air Force Historical Research Center: Corona Harvest Collection, 23 February 1972), 8.

15. O. P. Weyland, Report 168.7104-101—"Talks by General Patton and General Weyland at Press Conference" (Albert F. Simpson Historical Research Center: Weyland Collection, 9 December 1944), 4–5.

16. Weyland, Report 168.7104-101—Press Conference, 16 December 1944, 4.

17. Charles M. Province, *Patton's Third Army: A Daily Combat Diary* (New York: Hippocrene Books, 1992), 290–91.

18. Stephenson, Report K239.0512-813, 22–23.

19. Ibid., 75–76.

20. F. W. Winterbotham, *The Ultra Secret* (New York: Harper & Row, 1974), 98.

21. F. H. Hinsley, *British Intelligence in the Second World War: Its Influence on Strategy and Operations* (New York: Cambridge University Press, 1979), 947–48.

22. Wladyslaw Kozaczuk, *Enigma: How the German Machine Cipher Was Broken, and How It Was Read by the Allies in World War Two* (Frederick, Md.: University Publications of America, 1984), 24.

23. Edward Hitchcock, "The Hut Six Story," *Foreign Intelligence Literary Scene*, June 1982, 77.

24. Ibid.

25. Alfred McCormack, SRH-185—"War Experiences of Alfred McCormack" (National Archives: Record Group 457, 31 July 1947), 10–11.

26. Melvin C. Helfers, Personal Papers—"My Personal Experience with High Level Intelligence" (Charleston, S.C.: The Citadel Archives, November 1974), 8.

27. Ibid.

28. McCormack, 4.

29. Thomas Parrish, *The American Codebreakers: The US Role in ULTRA* (Chelsea, Mich.: Scarborough Press, 1991), 187.

30. Ibid., 189.

31. Helfers, 3.

32. Oscar W. Koch and Robert G. Hays, *G-2 Intelligence for Patton* (Philadelphia: Whitmore Publishing Co., 1971), xvi.

33. Helfers, 1.

34. Ibid., 10.

35. Melvin C. Helfers, video tape interview at The Citadel (Charleston, S.C.: The Citadel Archives, 16 October 1984).

36. Harry M. Grove, SRH-023—"Reports by US Army ULTRA Representatives in the European Theater of Operations" (National Archives: Record Group 457, 30 May 1945), 2–3.

37. Ibid., 3.

38. Helfers, Personal Papers, 8.

39. Koch and Hays, 147.

40. Grove, 4.

41. Roger H. Nye, *The Patton Mind: The Professional Development of an Extraordinary Leader* (Garden City Park, N.Y.: Avery Publishing, 1993), 67 and 102.

42. Omar N. Bradley, *A Soldier's Story* (New York: Henry Holt Co., 1951), 33.

43. Fred Ayer Jr., *Before the Colors Fade* (Boston: Houghton Mifflin, 1964), 175.

44. John C. Griggs, SRH-023—"Reports by US Army ULTRA Representatives in the European Theater of Operations" (National Archives: Record Group 457, 17 May 1945), 1.

45. Adolph G. Rosengarten Jr., SRH-023—"Reports by US Army ULTRA Representatives in the European Theater of Operations" (National Archives: Record Group 457, 21 May 1945), 7.

46. SRH-113—"ULTRA History of the US Strategic Air Force Europe versus German Air Forces" (National Archives: Record Group 457, May 1945), 4–5.

47. Helfers, Personal Papers, 10.

48. Warrack Wallace, SRH-108—"Report on Assignment with the Third United States Army 15 August–18 September 1944" (National Archives: Record Group 457, 21 May 1945), 3–4.

49. George C. Church, SRH-023—"Reports by US Army ULTRA Representatives in the European Theater of Operations" (National Archives: Record Group 457, 28 May 1945), 4.

50. Helfers, Personal Papers, 2.

51. Province, 12.

52. Third US Army, "After Action Report, 1 Aug 44–9 May 45," vol. 1, Annex 4: Third US Army Outline Plan, Regensburg, Germany, 1945, 1. Copy located in Auburn University Library, Auburn, Ala.

53. Ibid., 1–2.

54. Carlo D'Este, *Patton: A Genius for War* (New York: HarperCollins Publishers, 1995), 622.

55. Helfers, video tape interview.

56. Robert S. Allen, *Lucky Forward* (New York: Vanguard Press, 1947), 68.

57. Third US Army, "After Action Report, 1 Aug 44–9 May 45," vol. 1, Annex N, Third US Army Directives, Regensburg, Germany, 1945 , I–VII. Copy located in Auburn University Library, Auburn, Ala.

58. D'Este, 617.

59. Ibid., 614.

Chapter 3

Breakout in Brittany

Patton studied every ULTRA signal and, knowing where every enemy soldier was in his path, would thread his way round or through them and find the undefended spot. He had done it in Sicily and then all the way from Brittany to the Rhine.

—Group Capt F. W. Winterbotham
Senior ULTRA officer

The conditions that existed in August 1944 could not have been more conducive to Patton's style of warfare. The French countryside was littered with thinly manned German units who were trying to guess where the Allies would strike next. Throughout June and July, the Allies employed Patton as a decoy. This ruse helped convince the Germans that Patton's nonexistent First US Army Group (FUSAG) would lead the *grossen* invasion at Calais, an area 200 miles northeast of the Allied beachheads. As the Fifteenth German Army idly watched the D-day invasions awaiting the main attack from FUSAG at Calais, the Third US Army was busy planning its maneuvers to exploit the sparse German force allocations on the Brittany Peninsula.

Patton's Playground

The original D-day plans called for the entire Third Army to be committed to Brittany. Its first mission was the reduction of the peninsula, and then its four corps would be "concentrated in preparation for operations to the east."[1] Insight into the dire German circumstances would dictate modifications to the initial D-day plans and greatly reduce the Third Army's commitment to the Brittany Peninsula. Increased insight into German operations by August also greatly aided Patton's design for maneuver warfare. On 20 July 1944, Adolf Hitler narrowly escaped an

25

assassination attempt that significantly shook his confidence in the German military. With the trust of the German military undermined, Hitler decided to direct the war increasingly from his headquarters. His orders would not escape the attention of the Allied ULTRA analysts who would often take action on these directives as quickly as their intended recipients—hence further centralization of German command-aided Allied understanding of dispositions and intentions.

Patton's version of blitzkrieg warfare greatly aided the ULTRA effort. His rapid pursuits, encirclements, and deep thrusts rarely allowed the Germans to employ hardwire communications. Therefore, the increasingly mobile German troops became more reliant on the wireless Enigma machine for the majority of their communication needs. This fact became clear to the Bletchley Park officials who saw the sharp increase in ULTRA traffic soon after Patton's forces broke out of Normandy. Ralph Bennett, a senior intelligence officer at Bletchley Park, described this phenomenon of the summer of 1944: "The volume of traffic dropped when the front became temporarily stabilized soon after the fall of Cherbourg [end of June] and was slow to pick up again until Cobra brought about a resumption of mobile warfare a month later and raised the traffic-levels to unprecedented heights . . . Mercifully, the famine began to abate as Cobra got under way and August was once more a time of plenty."[2] The vast amounts of information dictated that any future Third Army campaign must exploit the advantages associated with an enfeebled enemy. Many of these ULTRA messages made it very apparent that the Germans were extremely vulnerable to a rapid air-ground attack.

The XIX TAC also saw August 1944 as a time of opportunity. The battle for air superiority clearly had been won by the Allies, and the summer days were conducive to exploiting this newly gained leverage in the air. Although the Third Army and the XIX TAC would not become officially operational until 1 August 1944, XIX TAC had been flying sorties with IX Fighter Command since February 1944 and found the summer months propitious for an air campaign. One after-action report included this statement: "taking full advantage of the long summer days, some groups flew as many as five separate missions in one day, and many pilots put in a 'working day' of more than 12 hours of almost continuous fighter-bombing."[3] When the XIX TAC moved to forward airfields, weather problems such as morning fog on the peninsula were negated, which also increased sortie generation rates. The Third Army's advance captured airfields so rapidly that XIX TAC moved its combat headquarters five times in August.[4] Like ULTRA, ground action aided the air campaign. Although moving to new air bases tested the command and control of XIX TAC operations, these bases afforded decreased fuel consumption and time-to-target rates while increasing target loiter times and sortie generation. Overall, Patton's forces soon found out in early August that the ground scheme of maneuver, ULTRA, and airpower were mutually beneficial.

The XIX TAC was not the only unit operating before the formal 1 August 1944 start date. Patton had unofficially been directing Gen Troy Middleton's VIII Corps since 28 July, and some of his orders were causing some consternation among the veteran hedgerow fighters. The official US Army history of World War II captures some of the problems Middleton encountered when General Bradley transferred his corps from First to Third Army: "Middleton, methodical and meticulous, found himself in a whirlwind that threatened to upset his ideas of an orderly and controlled progress. The transfer of VIII Corps from First to Third Army brought changes in staff procedures, communications, and supply, but these were minor problems compared to exigencies that emerged in rapid succession as a result of positional warfare in Cotentin to wide-open exploitation in Brittany."[5] First Army tended to emphasize formal staff work, often committing its plans to paper and requiring precise reports from subordinate units. Patton favored the opposite end of the spectrum. He advocated a "good plan violently executed now rather than a perfect plan next week"; and for Patton, staff planning and orders were frequently conducted through informal briefings and conversations.[6]

Middleton, an infantryman, was not the only one who perceived some of the new cavalry-minded orders as perplexing. Weyland's staff reported "General Patton's first request to

Nineteenth TAC was a strange one: do not blow up any bridges."[7] In the past, this technique was effective for slowing German movements; but Patton looked at interdiction another way. He wanted the bridges so his forces could move without delay. Patton's plans were built on high-speed movement. His plan was to prevent movements "from, not to" the battle area, in order to keep the lines of communication (LOC) ahead of his troops as smooth and as fluid as possible.[8]

The XIX TAC also had some transition problems associated with the transfer from First to Third Army, as noted by XIX TAC pilots:

> Before Cobra, the second priority assignment for air as the First Army fought stubbornly from hill to hill and patiently stormed strong points, was to attack German defensive positions which had held out for days and might hold out for weeks. Thunderbolts would plan, twenty-four to forty-eight hours in advance, to dive bomb a tough machine gun concentration or fort impregnable from ground. In Third Army–Nineteenth TAC tactics, the second job too was reversed. There were no such things as German "strong points" in Brittany short of the great island and port fortresses. Over the open country of the peninsula, the Germans rarely paused long enough to make a stand at Hill X or Ridge Y. It became impossible to plan tactical support missions a day in advance, when Third Army tanks rolled ahead twenty miles a day and when aircraft had to make sure, before an attack, that the objective had not already been taken out by our ground forces. All these considerations added up to the same thing. In support of Gen. Patton, Nineteenth TAC would find its targets in the field, and would plan as it flew.[9]

The XIX TAC found one of the best ways to support the above operations was through dedicated armor cover, which at the time was considered by the Air Corps to be an inefficient use of airpower. The standard procedure for this operation was to fly 35 miles ahead of the column to seek out and destroy strong points or pockets of resistance that might hamper forward movement.[10] The XIX TAC also found itself performing a myriad of unconventional tasks ranging from flank support for the entire Third Army to covering and defending bridges for ground troops or simply reporting the present location of Patton spearheads.

Patton's preparations for his upcoming operations in Brittany appeared unorthodox to many members of his command. The majority of these changes concerned air-ground cooperation, and it was clear throughout Patton's organization that any procedure that did not emphasize speed or the rapid advance of the Third Army would not survive the general's scrutiny.

Combat Operations Begin

The front that Patton inherited on 1 August afforded a tenuous gateway into Brittany. One of the greatest limiting factors for Patton during this time was getting his forces through a bottleneck at Avranches. Avranches is a small town between the See and Selune Rivers, and movement along the few roads that went through the town had to be managed with great precision (map 1). One task force with 3,500 men was instructed to arrive "in Avranches precisely at 0200 . . . not before and was to clear Pontaubault exactly by 0500." (See map 2, example 1.)[11] This task was so challenging that it led Patton to comment in his diary on 1 August: "Visited the VIII Corps to coordinate the movement of the 90th Division through the rear areas. This is an operation which, at Leavenworth, would certainly give you an unsatisfactory mark, as we are cutting the 90th Division through the same town and on the same street being used by two armored and two other infantry divisions. However, there is no other way of doing it at this time."[12] The criticality of Avranches was noted by both sides, and many orders during the month of August focused on the destruction or protection of this vital choke point.

On 1 August Patton's G-2, Colonel Koch, also provided possible enemy reactions to the oncoming Third Army attacks. The assessment stated that the Germans could "launch a major armored counterattack against the Army's east flank designed to drive a wedge to the sea and sever the north-south supply line."[13] It also estimated that the enemy could evacuate to the south and west while delaying by using favorable terrain for sporadic defense, or "he could withdraw into and defend the heavily fortified Brittany ports."[14] The first week of fighting in Brittany would see the Germans attempt to execute each option listed in Koch's report. Patton wasted no time in preparing Third Army units to counter these anticipated enemy countermoves.

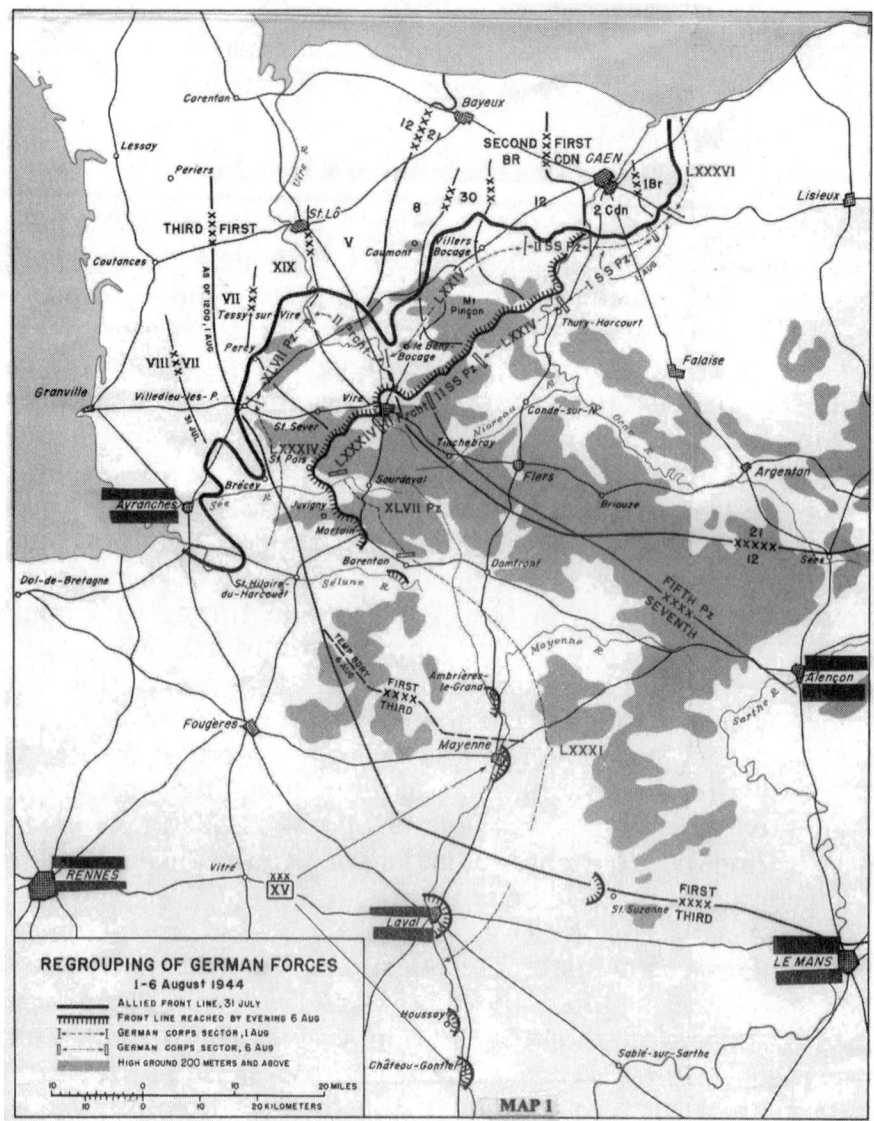

Map 1. Choke Point at Avranches

One of the first requests from Patton for the XIX TAC noted in General Weyland's diary called for "air cover over bridges and dams, as they are vulnerable and their destruction would cause debacle."[15] On 3 August Third Army specifically asked

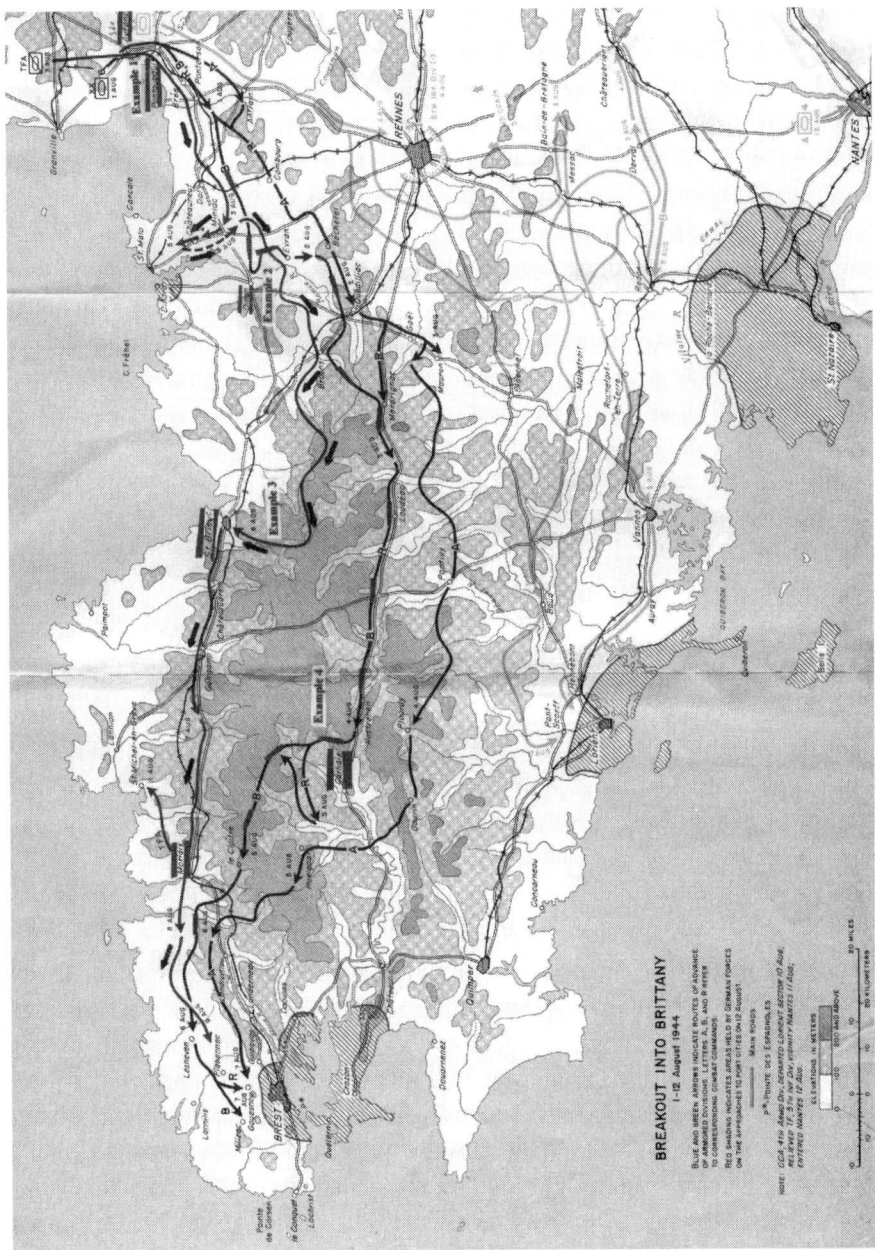

Map 2. Third Army Operations in Brittany

for fighter cover over the Pontorson bridge.[16] Due to vulnerabilities associated with Third Army's initial precarious posi-

31

tion, Weyland took these rear-area missions over Avranches and Pontorson seriously. As soon as XIX TAC received its first P-51 Mustangs, they were assigned to keep a constant fighter umbrella over the Third Army rear areas.[17]

Through ULTRA, Patton and the XIX TAC knew the Germans wanted to target vulnerable areas such as bridges and LOCs with any asset available. On 1 August at 2230 hours, the Germans transmitted an attack order to 116 Panzer Division instructing them to "hold their position and counter thrust towards Avranches."[18] The areas along the Allies' narrow LOCs were also a favorite for the German artillery, and Luftwaffe air tasking orders (ATO) continuously highlighted a focus on these LOCs. During this period the Allies consistently had access to German ATOs, which may help to answer von Rundstedt's initial question to Weyland during the former's subsequent interrogation: "How could you be everywhere all the time?"[19] During this period *Jagdkorps* Two continually called for "road strafing in Avranches" and "Schwerpunkt roads [are at] Avranches . . . Pontorson."[20] XIX TAC actively employed assets to counter both the German air and ground threats in this area. By midmorning 1 August, the Germans were introduced to the new air-ground team in-theater when the German commanders received reports stating: "that the Americans were at Pontorson and Dol-de-Bretagne and that two batteries of a German assault gun brigade committed against the armored spearheads had been destroyed principally by fighter-bombers."[21]

Although the first day's activities had many successes, there were some initial problems associated with the transition from static to mobile warfare. Late in the first day, General Patton received a report that a German armor column was headed for Third Army spearheads. Patton quickly tasked Weyland to intercept it, and the XIX TAC "put three groups of F/B (fighter/bombers) on the German column."[22] Patton later recalled this episode as very amusing as he related the following story: "I asked General Weyland . . . to send some fighter bombers to stop it. The bombers were unable to find the column, because it actually was the 4th Armored Division moving in from the northeast. However, the planes did do some effective work knocking out enemy resistance ahead of the 4th Armored Division and this was a precursor of many other such jobs. It was love at first sight between the XIX Tactical Air Command and the Third Army."[23]

Patton's rapid advances often put timely information about the current situation at a premium. This is why capabilities like ULTRA could be especially valuable in a high-speed campaign. During this drive, Patton committed the 6th and 4th Armored Divisions and divided each division into three combatant commands: CC A, CC B, and CC R reserve. Due to a change in priorities, a reduced effort was committed to Brittany, leaving the task that was once for the entire Third Army to VIII Corps.[24] Although this force did not have the originally planned firepower, Patton was interested in speed; and these lighter commands could efficiently exploit the confusion that existed within the German units. On 2 August ULTRA found one unit in Dinan that correctly estimated the strength of 6th Armor's CC B when it reported the Allies were "attacking Dinan but without strong forces," and the message then referred to a "German attack from east to west on Dinan."[25] Dinan was quickly identified as a German strong point and was bypassed (map 2, example 2). It is not surprising that at noon on the 4th, Patton issued the order "Dinan will not, repeat, not be attacked."[26] It is also not surprising that at 2130 hours that same day, a German commander submitted a message complaining "Dinan sector no repeat no contact with Allies."[27]

Another unit that bypassed Dinan was the even lighter Task Force A. Patton specifically created this force of 3,500 men to support the attack on Brest through the rapid capture of bridges from the north. Although the force was initially diverted to St. Malo by the VIII Corps commander, Patton interceded because he wanted "Task Force A to sweep the north coast of Brittany."[28] ULTRA information from 4 August suggested the north roads of Brittany were primed for Task Force A. At 1115 on 4 August, the German naval harbor master at St. Brieuc reported that the "[Kriegsmarine] had blown up and abandoned its bases."[29] Further confirmation came on 5 August when a report on St. Brieuc claimed "the infantry had moved off, base blown up."[30] Task Force A quickly secured that town on the 6th, and ULTRA messages received early that same day gave Task Force A little reason to deviate from the road leading out of St. Brieuc. On 5 August the German 266th Division reported forces "between St. Brieuc and Morlaix with few divisional troops and three Ost Battalions of little fighting value and limited mobility."[31] The message proved accurate. On 9 August Task Force A reported they had completed their mission with few losses and had encountered very few enemy soldiers (map 2, example 3).[32]

ULTRA was not the only source of information during this campaign. Sixth Armored Division's CC B was traveling on the main road that paralleled the north highway that Task Force A used, when suddenly the French Forces of the Interior warned that 2,000 paratroopers were to make a defense at Carhaix.[33] Early in the morning of the 5th, CC B was directed to bypass Carhaix. During that same morning, an ULTRA message arrived confirming the location of the paratroopers and their frustration because at Carhaix there was "no repeat no contact with the Allies, [Germans sent] Reece in easterly direction." [34] (See map 2, example 4.)

The key to operations in Brittany was the concept of avoiding strong points and exploiting the weak areas of the German defenses. Unfortunately, Brittany was also the home of numerous fortresses that overlooked many of the key ports that the Allies wanted to use in the coming winter months. Prior to the D-day invasion, there were numerous reports on these fortresses, most of which revealed that they would not be easy to conquer. Strangely, the Japanese were a great source of information on this topic. The Japanese ambassador in Berlin, Gen Oshima Hiroshi, dutifully reported back to Tokyo often enough to become one section of Grove's standard briefing headings under the category of "Special Information."[35] Carl Boyd, in *Hitler's Japanese Confidant*, captures the information that Hitler shared with this general which was transmitted back to Tokyo and intercepted by the Allies. General Oshima described the improvements to these forts (caliber of guns, rates of fire, disposition of forces, etc.) that began in 1942 and which made clear that these forts would not fall quickly to

Allied pressure.[36] His information was considered so important that President Franklin D. Roosevelt was provided a copy of the intercepted messages.[37]

ULTRA reports early in the campaign also confirmed German attachment to these fortresses. ULTRA intercepted orders to the commander of St. Milo directing "that suitable vessels [are] to be employed to support artillery fire in order to use everything to hold St. Milo."[38] On 4 and 5 August, XIX TAC "braved solid flak" and destroyed and damaged some of these ships; but the fort's defensive walls were beyond the capabilities of the fighter-bomber of 1944.[39] Hitler invested much in these fortresses, hoping that the Allies would tie up troops attacking garrisons as opposed to fighting their way into Germany. Hitler selected dependable commanders for these fortifications, required them to take an oath to defend to the death, and specifically ordered them to hold these forts "to the last man, to the last cartridge."[40] The Allies knew these fortresses would not be easy to take, but their biggest question was how long the Germans would delay in Brittany before they retreated back to their strongholds east of the Rhine.

Attacks on these forts would have given the Germans time to build up defensive positions on other areas of the peninsula. Twelfth Army Group understood this quickly and directed on 2 August that "St. Malo may be bypassed and contained if reduction takes too large a force and too much time."[41] Time and large forces were not items the Allies had, and Patton was content to let the Germans bottle themselves in these fortresses. Early morning on the 6th, ULTRA provided another confirmation on what fortresses were of the greatest concern to the Germans when they directed their forces "available in Brittany to be concentrated in the fortresses of St. Malo, Brest, Lorient, and St. Nazaire."[42] That same day, 12th Army Group provided the assessment "Enemy resistance in Brittany now consists of scattered pockets and port garrisons apparently to defend St. Nazaire, Lorient, Brest, and the Peninsula North of Guingamp."[43] A captured German general best describes the Allies' strategy during this phase when he accuses Hitler of having fortress mania: "The enemy was content simply to keep these fortresses under observation, since they could do no harm to his conduct of the campaign as a whole. But they cost us between 160,000 and 200,000 men, together with costly weapons and equipment."[44]

The above facts rapidly made Brittany a backwater operation, and Patton's attention quickly turned to the east. Patton knew he had a small window of opportunity to exploit the confusion that existed within the German lines, and the attacks on St. Malo and Brest would have to wait as the 4th Armored Division sealed off the Brittany Peninsula.

Initially, the drive to Brittany was focused on securing additional ports for logistical support and reducing the strain on the Normandy beaches. The rapid withdrawal of the German forces to their fortresses and the void of German forces eastward changed the Allies' priorities. Gen Dwight D. Eisenhower reflected the Allies' attitude towards Brittany's ports when he said: "any attempt to capture the place [main port of Brest] in a single assault would be extremely costly to us. Fortunately, our prospects for securing better ports than Brest began to grow much brighter just before the middle of August."[45] The ports Eisenhower referred to were farther east, and he noted "the distance from Brest to the Metz region was greater than the distance from Marseille (southern France) to Metz."[46] The rapid gains of the Allied armies quickly made Brittany's ports a secondary priority.

Overall, as soon as the German forces were bottled up in their fortresses, the Allies' rear areas were relatively secure. Further efforts against these German troops would become a waste of resources at a critical time period. Patton understood this as he turned his attention towards Paris and the exploitable French countryside.

The Lure from the East

The Allied attacks farther inland did not have to tackle fortresses; and the topography east of Brittany was devoid of many natural barriers, which made this region conducive to rapid armor thrusts. ULTRA also pointed out through numerous messages that the positions in this sector were weakly manned, which enticed the Allies to drive east before the

Germans could rectify the situation. Although it appeared from initial indications that Rennes would be a German strong point, on 2 August ULTRA showed a different picture. Early in the morning of 2 August, the Allies received an intercepted message that instructed Germans on 1 August in Rennes to "begin at once" the destruction of Rennes.[47] It appeared the Germans did not have long-term plans for this city, and on 3 August, "elements of the 8th Infantry Division captured Rennes over light enemy resistance."[48]

Farther to the east and south, even more revealing messages were received that provided insight into the desperate situation in the German rear areas. On 1 and 2 August, reports from Laval requested "supply columns to be sent at once to Laval . . . Supply of fighting troops no longer possible" and they also needed "M/T [motor transport] . . . for evacuation."[49] On the 2d, LeMans (farther to the east) cried for "35 medium lorries immediately, otherwise [there is a] danger that irreplaceable equipment might have to be blown up."[50] There were numerous indicators that German defenses were ill prepared for an Allied drive to the east, and Patton did not want to give his adversaries any time to correct their situation. On the 4th, he gave orders for XV Corps "to seize the bridgehead at Laval . . . [then] to LeMans and prepare for further action to the north or east or northeast."[51] (See map 1.)

During these drives Third Army continued to receive confirmation through ULTRA of thinly manned German positions. Patton quickly determined that this situation needed to be exploited. On the morning of 5 August, an ULTRA message revealed that the Germans had scheduled "withdrawal operations Gruppe from Laval . . . envisioned for night 5th/6th."[52] On the 6th, patrols discovered that the German garrison was thoroughly destroyed; and the following morning they found Laval had been evacuated and met no opposition securing the town (see map 1).[53] Similar situations occurred with other small towns, but Patton was only interested in driving as far south as the Loire River, with the next southern target being Angers.

As Patton's forces were driving towards Angers on the 7th, ULTRA reported that the previous day the following order went to German units: "Angers . . . to be destroyed as soon as no more units on them. Transfers to be made rapidly."[54] Later that day Patton "verbally ordered the XX Corps to move one regimental combat team from 5th Infantry Division to Angers" and on 10 August "Angers was captured without resistance."[55] (See map 3.) The preparatory air attacks on LeMans and Angers represented some of the complexities of striking targets based purely on ULTRA information. Because only a few officers were indoctrinated into ULTRA, sometimes line pilots were very frustrated with what they viewed as worthless missions. One ULTRA officer recounted this problem with the following story:

> Through this recipient's ULTRA-inspired recommendations, repeated attacks were made against the clutches of fields at Alencon, LeMans, Angers, etc. Invariably, pilots would return from these missions reporting "no aircraft seen" and somewhat "browned off" at dumping their eggs on apparently inactive fields and dispersal areas. Regular as clockwork, however, SOURCE [ULTRA] would produce a reaction such as, "Ten a/c [aircraft] lost from low level attack," "No serviceable a/c left," "All technical flying equipment heavily shot up," "impossible to occupy airfield any longer," etc. Even Operations, non-indoctrinated at the time, was skeptical, but the Air Commander continued to back the program because he knew they were there and were being affected by the effort. Eventually, a IX pilot was shot down over one of the Angers strips and lay for days in the woods where he watched the German fighters take-off and land throughout the daylight hours and he observed their careful camouflage and dispersal systems. On his return to Allied lines he told of having been mentally gripped at the time of his attack because he could see no aircraft and thought he was performing a wasteful and useless mission. His eyewitness account did much to boost morale and obtain confidence in the advocated program.[56]

The initial phase of this campaign saw a dramatic transition from the tough fighting in the hedgerows under the First Army to Patton's rapid advances throughout Brittany and his first strides towards Paris. Patton's program, however, took time to gain the confidence of all participants; and it also experienced growing pains. From the XIX TAC being tasked to intercept a friendly armored column or the initial request to "not bomb bridges" to the realization that air liaison officers were needed below division and corps level, all these details needed to be worked out to ensure Patton's operational methods could be employed.

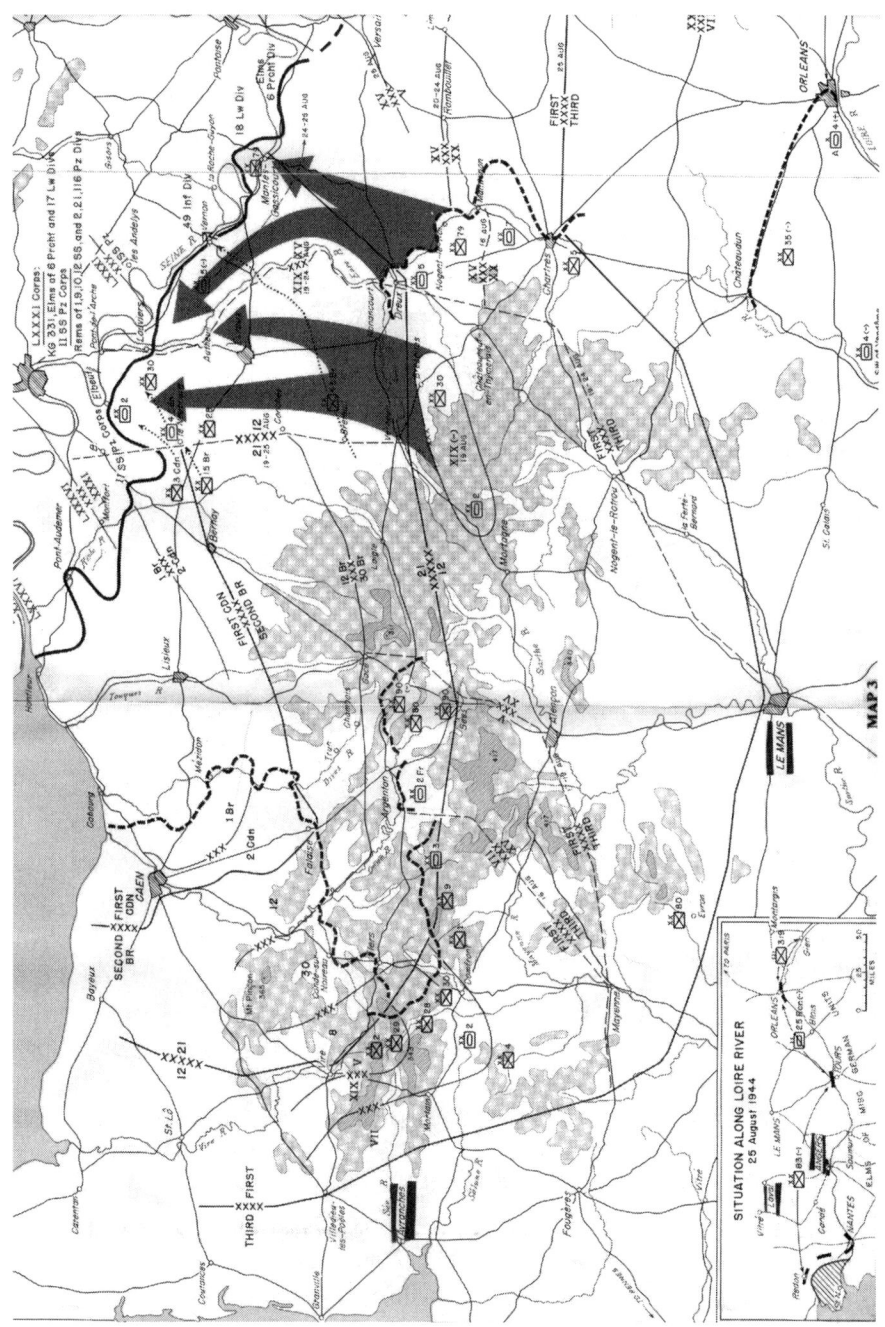

Map 3. Angers and the Breakout Area

Middleton also found his new commander's methods unorthodox; and Patton sometimes had to overturn some of his subordinate's more cautious orders, one time muttering to himself "and he was a good doughboy, too."[57] There was no doubt that Patton's operational approach was controversial, and some authors still criticize his methods claiming "principally, he occupied ground rather than destroying armies."[58] Unfortunately, what Middleton and these critics did not understand was that if Third Army slowed down to destroy the enemy, it would provide other areas time to prepare defenses—a fact later realized in the fall of 1944. Patton understood that rapid drives to rear areas could force the enemy back into fortresses where they could be rendered useless. When his thrusts eventually did put him in a position to destroy an entire army, he was stopped repeatedly by higher headquarters.

During this phase of the operation, Patton employed many nonstandard schemes to exploit the conditions in Brittany. This phase successfully tested many of the force enhancers that would carry Patton across the French countryside. ULTRA, airpower, and the ground scheme of maneuver were mutually complementary. ULTRA revealed the German strong points; and Patton crafted a ground scheme of maneuver that avoided these areas in order to capture territory, which forced many Germans either to surrender or retreat back to their fortresses. ULTRA also informed Patton on the capabilities of those fortresses; and Patton merely chose not to attack them, preferring to leave these German troops as prisoners behind their own walls. In the cases of Avranches and Pontaubault, ULTRA reconfirmed the threats to these areas. In these instances Patton knew he had to defend these areas, while the Germans often provided their attack plans to him through ULTRA.

Patton's ground scheme of maneuver facilitated ULTRA by forcing the retreating Germans away from wire communications and into reliance on the wireless Enigma machine. Once these German forces arrived at their fortresses, the communication lines were cut by the Allies' siege troops. This act ensured accurate ULTRA information on the blockaded fortresses for the remainder of the war. The ground scheme of maneuver also aided the air campaign by capturing German airfields. These new fields allowed airpower to be rapidly applied on the battlefield, and it also secured areas away from the unfavorable weather conditions associated with peninsulas.

Similarly, airpower assisted the ground scheme through CAS and interdiction that ensured the rapid advances of Third Army. Airpower was also used to release troops that may have been dedicated to secure rear areas and allowed them to exploit the fluid situation in Brittany. These fluid conditions were fertile grounds for ULTRA, which fed information back into this system; and Patton's force-enhancing program soon had a momentum of its own. Patton would need all of these advantages for the upcoming battle because the Allies were soon to experience their first major counterattack on the European continent.

Notes

1. Third US Army, "After Action Report, 1 Aug 44–9 May 45," vol. 1, Annex 4, Third US Army Outline Plan, Regensburg, Germany, 1945, 1. Copy located in Auburn University Library, Auburn, Ala.

2. Ralph F. Bennett, *ULTRA in the West: The Normandy Campaign, 1944–45* (New York: Scribner, 1980), 101.

3. XIX TAC Staff, Report 168.7104-101—"Fly, Seek, and Destroy" (Albert F. Simpson Historical Research Center: Weyland Collection, 13 December 1944), 2.

4. XIX TAC Staff, Report 168.7104-81—"Planes over Patton" (Albert F. Simpson Historical Research Center: Weyland Collection, 30 October 1944), 1.

5. Martin Blumenson, *Breakout and Pursuit* (Washington, D.C.: Office of the Chief of Military History, Department of the Army, 1961), 350.

6. Ibid., 344–45.

7. XIX TAC Staff, "Planes over Patton," 8.

8. Ibid.

9. XIX TAC Staff, "Planes over Patton," 8–9.

10. XIX TAC Staff, Report 168.7104-64—"Twelve Thousand Fighter-Bomber Sorties" (Albert F. Simpson Historical Research Center: Weyland Collection, 30 September 1944), 3.

11. Blumenson, 356.

12. Martin Blumenson, *The Patton Papers*, vol. 2, *1940–1945* (Boston: Houghton Mifflin, 1974), 495.

13. Third US Army, "After Action Report, 1 Aug 44–9 May 45," vol. 1, Third US Army August Operations, Regensburg, Germany, 1945, 16. Copy located in Auburn University Library, Auburn, Ala.

14. Ibid.

15. O. P. Weyland, Report 168.7104-1—"Weyland Diary—XIX TAC" (Albert F. Simpson Historical Research Center: Weyland Collection, 18 May 1945), diary, 1 August 1944, entry 2030 hours.

16. Ibid., 3 August 1944, entry 1900 hours.

17. XIX TAC Staff, "Planes over Patton," 16.

18. Great Britain Public Record Office, "ULTRA: Main Series of Signals Conveying Intelligence," Bletchley Park, 1944, reel 33, XL 4499. Copy located in Auburn University Library, Auburn, Ala.

19. O. P. Weyland, Report 168.7104-95—"Weyland's Interrogation of von Rundstedt at Bad Kissingen" (Albert F. Simpson Historical Research Center: Weyland Collection, 2 July 1945), 6.

20. Great Britain Public Record Office, reel 34, XL 4626 and XL 4759.

21. Blumenson, *Breakout and Pursuit*, 341.

22. "Weyland Diary—XIX TAC," 1 August, entry 2030 hours.

23. George S. Patton Jr., Paul D. Harkins, and Beatrice A. Patton, *War as I Knew It* (Boston: Houghton Mifflin Co., 1947), 99.

24. Dwight D. Eisenhower, *Crusade in Europe* (Garden City, N.Y.: Doubleday, 1948), 274.

25. Great Britain Public Record Office, reel 34, XL 4482.

26. Blumenson, *Breakout and Pursuit*, 378.

27. Great Britain Public Record Office, reel 34, XL 4787.

28. Blumenson, *Breakout and Pursuit*, 389–91.

29. Great Britain Public Record Office, reel 34, XL 4681.

30. Ibid., XL 4860.

31. Ibid., XL 4912.

32. Blumenson, *Breakout and Pursuit*, 392.

33. Ibid., 379.

34. Great Britain Public Record Office, reel 34, XL 4798.

35. Harry M. Grove, SRH-023—"Reports by US Army ULTRA Representatives in the European Theater of Operations" (National Archives: Record Group 457, 30 May 1945), 2.

36. Carl Boyd, *Hitler's Japanese Confidant: General Oshima Hiroshi and Magic Intelligence, 1941–1945* (Lawrence, Kans.: University Press of Kansas, 1993), 189–90.

37. National Security Agency, Report 170.601-5—"Magic Reports for the Attention of the President" (Albert F. Simpson Historical Research Center: Special Collections, 1943–44), 1–17.

38. Great Britain Public Record Office, reel 34, XL 4444.

39. XIX TAC Staff, "Planes over Patton," 14.

40. Blumenson, *Breakout and Pursuit*, 340.

41. Third US Army, 12th Army Group Directives, 2.

42. Great Britain Public Record Office, reel 34, XL 4900.

43. Third US Army, 12th Army Group Directives, 2.

44. Seymour Freidin, Werner Kreipe, and William Richardson, eds., *The Fatal Decisions* (New York: W. Sloan Associates, 1956), 236.

45. Eisenhower, 280.

46. Ibid.

47. Great Britain Public Record Office, reel 34, XL 4375.

48. Third US Army, Third US Army August Operations, 18.

49. Great Britain Public Record Office, reel 34, XL 4325 and 4446.

50. Ibid., XL 4448.

51. Third US Army, Third US Army August Operations, 19.

52. Great Britain Public Record Office, reel 34, XL 4800.

53. Blumenson, *Breakout and Pursuit*, 434–44.

54. Great Britain Public Record Office, reel 34, XL 5046.

55. Third US Army, Third US Army August Operations, 22 and 26.

56. James D. Fellers, SRH-023—"Reports by US Army ULTRA Representatives in the European Theater of Operations" (National Archives: Record Group 457, 7 June 1945), 33.

57. Russell F. Weigley, *Eisenhower's Lieutenants: The Campaign of France and Germany, 1944–1945* (Bloomington, Ind.: Indiana University Press, 1981), 184.

58. Ibid., 245.

Chapter 4

Mortain Counteroffensive and the Falaise Gap

We must strike like lightning. When we reach the sea the American spearheads will be cut off. Obviously, they are trying all out for a major decision here because otherwise they would not have sent their best general, Patton. That's the most dangerous man they have. But the more troops they squeeze through the gap, and the better they are, the better for us when we reach the sea and cut them off!

—Adolf Hitler

The American victory in this battle appears as fine an example of improvisation, flexibility and courage. ULTRA had given the Allies . . . ample time to prepare exactly the right killing ground. Instead of stunned opponents scurrying to the rear, the Germans found a cool, poised and fully briefed reception committee.

—Ronald Lewin

Near the end of the first week of Third Army operations, Major Helfers saw his ULTRA AOR grow exponentially. As Helfers was supporting contingency planning for attacks driving east, west, and south, the most ominous clouds were rising over rear areas behind Third Army's forward command headquarters. During the first week of fighting, ULTRA messages clearly displayed the Germans' keen interest in the bottleneck at Avranches; and on 6 August, all indications predicted that this lifeline was soon to be threatened. One of the first messages Helfers received that morning made it apparent that the upcoming German action would be no small operation. The message highlighted *Jagdkorps* Two's response to the army that the "fighter operations as requested at the lowest strength requires employment of 1000 aircraft in one day in a limited area."[1] Although *Jagdkorps* Two declared "support in the manner requested is impossible," they provided the location of where their limited support would occur by stating the focus was "intended in [the] southern part of [the] area in question."[2] Five Z messages (the highest on the ULTRA priority scale) continued throughout the day, which later provided Helfers the exact details of the impending German attack in the "southern" area in question.

"To the Sea"—Targeting the Third Army Lifeline

At 1912 hours, ULTRA provided another Luftwaffe associated message from 2d *Schutzstaffeln* (*SS*) Panzer Division requesting "night fighter operations for protection of own [2 *SS* Panzer's] attack over area St. Clement–St. Hilaire and day fighters on the 7th for the same area."[3] (See map 4.) Twenty minutes later, another message was transmitted to the 47th Panzer Corps discussing an attack to the west with an attack formation "from right to left—116 Panzer Division, 2d Panzer Division, 1st *SS* Panzer Division and 2d *SS* Division."[4] By 2030 hours, ULTRA indications of impending enemy action became so ominous that Helfers believed they required Patton's immediate attention.

The 2d SS Panzer Division provided Helfers the location for the assault. It ordered an "attack on Mortain and [then a] thrust to St. Hilaire," and the message also made it easy for Allied aircraft interdicting these forces because it tasked the following identification procedure: "Ground troops [German] shooting green, designation of German aircraft by recognition signals."[5] However, an additional message that arrived later that evening made the biggest impression on Helfers: "At about eight that evening Captain Hutchinson (British liaison—Officer-in-charge of the ULTRA message center) came to my tent with a single long message. Hitler had ordered all armor units in the Caen area to assemble in a designated area and, as a mass, attack Mortain. Mortain was to be seized, the one American supply route from Normandy to northern France cut, and Americans south of Mortain killed or captured. That was getting too close to home, as the Third Army Headquarters was at that time south of Mortain."[6]

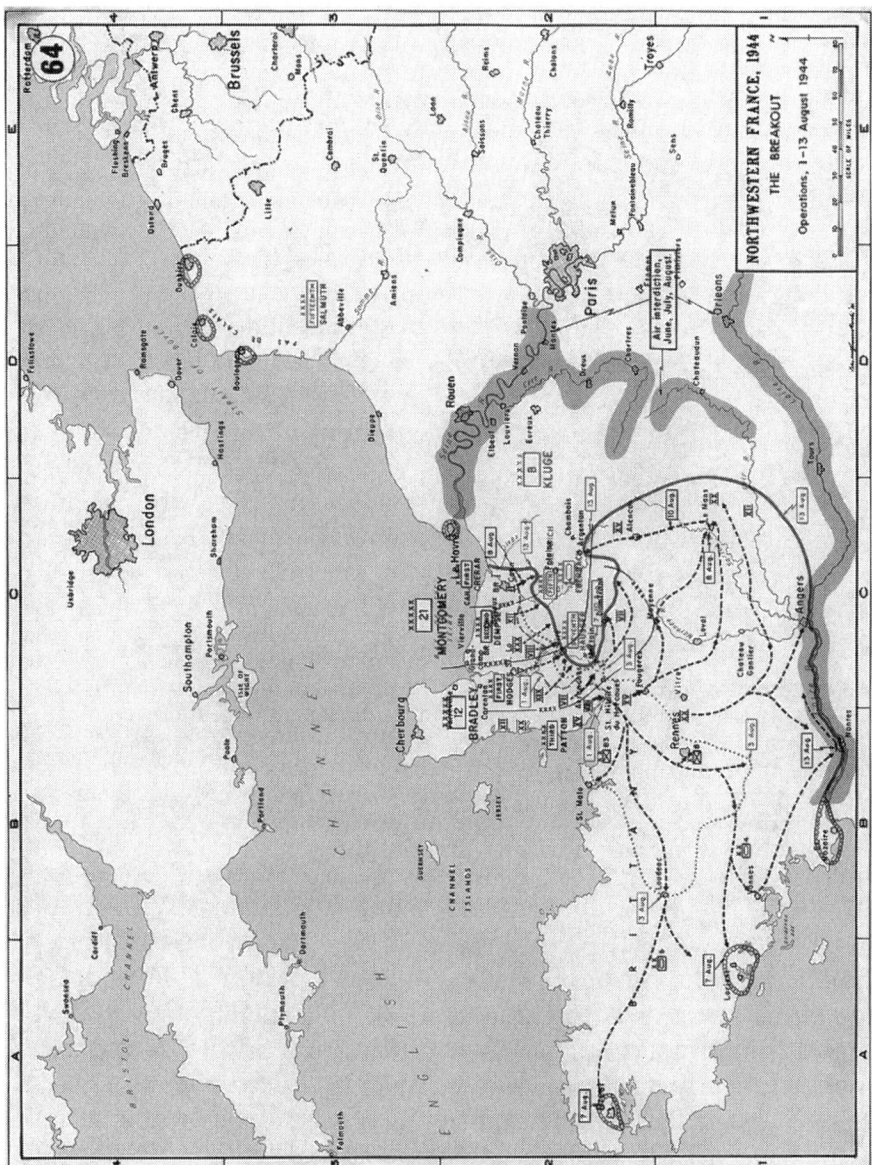

Map 4. Mortain and Falaise

Forty years later, Helfers still recalled this individual report and claimed "this is a good example of the high level important messages that came out of ULTRA intelligence"; and he further related his feelings on the night of 6 August:

> I remember this wording very well, these were the words of Hitler that came across ULTRA. [Helfers read the message.] "The outcome of the Battle of France depends on the success of the attack on the southern wing of the Seventh Army. Commander-in-Chief West will have a unique and unrepeatable opportunity of thrusting into the region largely devoid of the enemy, and to change the whole situation thereby." When I saw this message, I immediately felt that if General Patton doesn't get this message immediately—I'd be court-martialed.[7]

Helfers's actions began a chain of events that were corroborated by all senior officers involved; but because these officers died before the ULTRA secret was declassified, their guarded recollections of this event attribute the information to an unnamed source. As soon as Helfers finished transferring the contents of Hitler's message onto his map, he hurried with his charts, notes, and flashlight to find Colonel Koch. Helfers recalled, "Colonel Koch was in his tent dozing"; but after Helfers woke him up and went over the messages, "he [Koch] agreed that the Army Commander should receive the same intelligence at once."[8] Koch's 1971 book, *G-2: Intelligence for Patton,* used a similar but guarded account:

> Awakened by the intelligence section duty officer, I got answers. Word had just been received from higher headquarters, I was informed, that a "usually reliable source" had reported that a German counterattack of major proportions against First Army was imminent . . . noted that the XX Corps [of Third Army] was now moving south through the gap and that one of its divisions, the 35th was opposite the critical point. If the 35th were halted and turned toward the east . . . it would be in a position to backstop the First Army at the most threatened and most critical points. We'll go see the commander, Gay (Third Army Deputy Chief of Staff) decided.[9]

Helfers then had his first meeting with Patton. He was introduced as a major who had some special intelligence that required his immediate attention. Helfers spread his map on the floor, and the three officers informally squatted over the chart. Helfers showed how the one Five-Z message fit in with the rest of the other ULTRA messages displayed on the map. Patton did not immediately act on this information. Instead, he turned to Koch and asked what he thought of the data. Koch replied, "I think the source is genuine and fits the rest of the German situation."[10] Patton's previous intelligence experience taught him not to jump on single source intelligence, which is why he asked for Koch's opinion. Koch confirmed that his big picture (other sources of intelligence) corroborated the ULTRA depiction of the situation. Armed with this knowledge, Patton took immediate action. He phoned Maj Gen Walton Walker (commander, XX Corps), who was just passing through the Mortain bottleneck, and directed him to halt the corps's movement to the south and take up defensive positions facing east.[11] Patton's diary entry for the same period displayed his initial skepticism towards ULTRA when he wrote, "We got a rumor last night from a secret source that several panzer divisions will attack west from Mortain on Avranches. Personally, I think it is a German bluff to cover a withdrawal, but I stopped the 80th, French 2d Armor, and the 35th [Divisions] in the vicinity of St. Hilaire just in case something might happen."[12]

Patton's suspicions about this secret source are not surprising because this was his first real briefing from an ULTRA officer. Before this event, Third Army's standard ULTRA dissemination procedure was in the form of typewritten reports that were provided to Koch and then incorporated into the greater intelligence picture. This situation provided an opportunity for ULTRA information to attain greater significance at Third Army headquarters. Patton had placed some credence in Helfers's information, and the fate of an improved ULTRA program was dependent upon success at Mortain. Helfers did not have to wait long to find out that this was no "German bluff to cover a withdrawal"; and after this episode, Helfers became the only ULTRA officer to personally brief his commanding general on a daily basis.[13]

Soon after this initial ULTRA meeting, Helfers received additional confirmation of the impending German attack. Midnight brought a message ordering the Germans to attack "with strong forces of five panzer divisions from Sourdeval to Mortain towards the west, first objective road Brecey to Montigny" and *Jagdkorps* Two "to support [the] attack with all force except JIG Two."[14] Another message specifically mentioned Avranches and stated the "objective is to cut off Allies who have broken through to [the] south from supply base and to effect junction with the coast."[15] This information did not only affect planning at Third Army, these messages also had a corresponding ripple effect on XIX TAC. In his diary that same night, General Weyland wrote "Conference with Gen Gaffey (Third Army Chief of Staff) and Third Army staff reference possible German counterattack east to west between Selune and See."[16] Like Patton, Weyland took this information and started planning and coordinating with other units to create his version of a reception committee for the attacking Germans.

At 2300 hours Weyland made his final entry for 6 August, which stated "Missions laid on for 7 August, called Gen Q [Quesada, 9th TAC Commander] reference possible German counterattack. XIX TAC can divert F/B [fighter/bombers] to threaten area anytime—will coordinate between two TACs."[17] The coordination between these two TACs was facilitated by the fact that before Third Army became operational, XIX TAC's main focus was supporting First Army operations. Later that morning, additional plans were made to mass the effects of airpower to counter the German threat. These actions were also reflected in the following diary entry: "Gen Quesada requested use of 406 Group [P-47s] with rockets for easing pocket in the vicinity of Mortain and east to assist in the break up of hostile tank attacks, concurred . . . also agreed to put P-51 fighter cover over threatened area."[18] All of this planning resulted in a battle that clearly displayed the synergy that comes from efficient incorporation of ULTRA intelligence in a lethal air-ground campaign.

Early on the morning of 7 August, the attack came as expected. The Germans failed to find the "region largely devoid of the enemy" as Hitler had promised. Instead, they engaged dug-in divisions and a sky filled with tactical aircraft. Although the German forces made some initial gains, Allied forces quickly denied the enemy their objectives. Third Army ground preparations were handsomely rewarded. Koch recalled the decision to use Third Army as backstop forces was well founded when he stated, "The German counterattack came as expected. The 35th Division, later attached to the VII Corps of First Army for that action, became heavily engaged. Third Army troops continued to pour through the gap. The all-out German counterattack was not only repulsed, but the stage was set for the encirclement of the entire German Seventh Army in the Falaise area."[19] In this battle the

Germans got their first taste of concentrated Allied tactical air-power. They temporarily recaptured Mortain; but when the fog lifted, a murderous Allied air assault ensued. More than a thousand Allied fighter-bombers roamed the battlefield unchecked. Although *Jagdkorps* Two claimed it needed 1,000 planes for this battle, it could only muster 300; and by 8 August only 110 were still in action.[20]

XIX TAC found this battle fertile ground for increasing kill counts in every category. In the first week of operations, the XIX TAC did not log any enemy aircraft kills; but on 7 August they made up for lost time, chalking up 33 in one day. Preceding ULTRA messages had tracked retreating Luftwaffe aircraft to various bases in the rear, and the collateral secret account provided the following explanation for the day's high kill count: "part of the bag of enemy aircraft was obtained when information was received that Chartres airfield was ripe for attack."[21] XIX TAC's support to the battle did not stop with negating the German air threat; many of their more success-ful missions were ground attack sorties. One example comes from the unit that Weyland had transferred to Quesada the night before: "Tank battles were seen in the Vire–Mortain sec-tor, and our planes took a hand in them. In one attack, seven P-47s of the 405th Group claimed destruction of 12 tanks, five staff cars, four half-tracks (three of them carrying flak guns) and four light flak positions, plus damage to four other tanks."[22] Soon after the war, the Office of the Assistant Chief of Air Staff for Intelligence put out a report on this battle, sen-sationally stating that the Allies were "in danger of being cut off by a determined German counterattack at Avranches but the air ended this threat, pulverizing concentrations of enemy troops and armor as fast as they were formed."[23] Although this comment may exaggerate airpower's role in this engagement, it pales in comparison to the comments that came from the Germans.

In 1956 German Lt Gen Bodo Zimmerman (former chief op-erations officer, commander in chief [CINC] west, and Army Group D) recalled the battle stating, "After a certain initial success it was brought to a standstill at first light by the in-tervention of the Allied Air Force. This was the first time in history that an attacking force had been stopped solely by bombing."[24] XIX TAC and Third Army did not have to wait until 1956 to get the Germans' impression of the Allied air effort—by that afternoon, ULTRA reports immediately gave evidence of their success. The German Seventh Army reported "the actual attack had been at a standstill since 1300 hours, owing to the employment by the enemy of a great number of fighter-bombers and the absence of own aircraft."[25] Lower-echelon forces provided similar accounts. The 47th Panzer Corps claimed "the activity of fighter-bombers is said to be have been well-nigh unendurable" and 1st SS Panzer Division observed that they had "no previous experience of fighter-bomber attacks on this scale."[26] Although the Germans rightfully attributed much of the Allied success in this battle to airpower, it would be several years before they would learn that one of the greatest factors was ULTRA—a fact that was not missed by the Allied commanders involved.

Maj Warrack Wallace (Helfers's assistant) remembered the appreciation felt at Third Army for ULTRA by stating, "General Gaffey at a later date mentioned the Avranches incident to the writer [Wallace] as one of the cases in which the service [Ultra] had been invaluable."[27] This event also made a large impression on Bradley and Quesada. In 1977, when discussing the value of ULTRA, Quesada specifically brought up the Avranches: "You know, Brad and I never used to talk together about our ULTRA signals. We just took it for granted that each of us knew what was in them. But I can still see the moment when we stood with those signals in our hands, and grinned, and said we've got them."[28] Although the Allied commanders knew the secret to their success, the Germans never suspected a compromise of the Enigma message system. Therefore, they attributed their defeat to other factors. Considering that the Mortain counteroffensive was Hitler's plan, he had to find a scapegoat. The victim was CINC West *Generalfeldmarschall* Günther von Kluge. When the news of the fiasco reached Hitler, he ominously condemned Kluge with one sentence: "The attack failed because Kluge wanted it to fail."[29] Although Hitler permitted Kluge to command for another 11 days, the effects of this defeat ruined Kluge, which is reflected in his chief of staff's (Gen Günther Blumentritt) final memories of his commander:

> Kluge had been shocked by the failure of his counterattack on Avranches on August 7 and upset by Hitler's reproaches; he had sent his son into the Falaise pocket with the words "Let nobody accuse me of sparing my son and heir." . . . [Blumentritt] last saw him on the eighteenth, tapping a map chart and moaning, "Avranches, Avranches! This town has cost me my reputation as a soldier. I'll go down in history as the Benedeck (Austrian General crushed by Von Moltke in the Austro–Prussian War, 1866) of the western front. D'you know Count Moltke's book on Benedeck? I did my best but that's fate for you."[30]

Kluge never found out that his demise was less fate and more ULTRA. Soon after he left Blumentritt, he committed suicide by taking potassium cyanide on a roadside headed toward Metz.

Kluge was the first high-ranking victim of a truly integrated ULTRA, air, and ground operation. Lessons from North Africa and Sicily were coming to fruition in France, but Hitler thought he could correct the problem by changing commanders. The problem with this philosophy was that his solution would be a commander from the east who did not understand the capabilities of Allied airpower. Unfortunately for Hitler, the Allies in France were fully apprised of German strengths, weaknesses, and intentions. The Allies used airpower to attack all areas of the battlefield with a significant economy of force, which further exacerbated the German logistics and personnel problems that plagued the Western Front. The frustration with Hitler's simplistic solution for solving the problems on the western front (replacing Kluge with *Generalfeldmarschall* Walther Model) was best encapsulated by General Zimmerman: "Field Marshal Model, who had hitherto seen action only on the Eastern front, did not immediately grasp the full gravity of the situation in France and hoped that he might yet restore it. But he was soon to realize the unimaginable effects of the enemy's air supremacy, the massive destruction in the rear areas, the impossibility of traveling along any major road in daylight without great peril, in fact the full significance of the invasion."[31] Patton saw the opportunities ULTRA and airpower could provide, and he devised a new program to capitalize on the benefits that were afforded him during this campaign.

ULTRA Improvements at Third Army

Although Group Capt Winterbotham (a senior ULTRA officer) lauded the ULTRA influences at Patton's headquarters in Sicily, the ULTRA system before 6 August was greatly hindered by the representatives that were sent by Bletchley Park.[32] In Sicily the ULTRA representatives were British troops that did not fall under Patton's command, and their actions did little to improve Patton's apparent prejudice against his Anglo allies. In March 1944 the British and Americans agreed that US commands should brief their own commanders, but that the SLUs (message centers) would still be manned by British officers.[33] These troops were the responsibility of the G-2; and at Patton's headquarters, it was best to hide the British as best as possible. Helfers provided "a few thoughts about the British signal section" which would show why Koch concealed them.

> They were a pain in the neck to General Patton, I am sure, and they were a pain in the back to me. They were attached to Third Army headquarters, just as I was, and their records were administered somewhere else. Hence, nobody could tell them "nutt'in." They wore their uniforms as they pleased. They came and went as they pleased. They kept their quarters as they pleased and they cooked and ate as they pleased . . . The British captain's name by the way was Hutchinson, and he was a horse's a-- . . . I tried to win him over and even gave him a first-class dinner for him and the other three officers at the Bells of Peavor the night before Third Army headquarters left for Normandy, but no soap . . . So much for our gallant allies. Their intelligence was good but their attitude towards Americans was lousy as a rule.[34]

Helfers's military education from The Citadel taught him that sharp uniforms, spotless quarters, and being a member of the greater team were factors that were essential to success at Patton's headquarters. Unfortunately, his association with the British and the old procedures for ULTRA at Third Army still relegated Helfers's ULTRA inputs to typewritten pages that would be incorporated by Koch. But that all changed after Patton got off the phone directing General Walker to prepare for the counterattack on Avranches. Helfers's next story shows the necessity of having a competent and credible ULTRA sales-man at Patton's headquarters, which eventually transitioned the ULTRA input from one page of text into a comprehensive daily briefing:

> After telephoning, General Patton turned to me and asked me how long I had been with Third Army Headquarters and how valuable I thought the intelligence was that I was receiving from my source. I told him that since the Third Army had been operational, I had usually known twenty-four hours in advance what the Germans in front of Third Army units attempted to do. Thereupon, General Patton turned to Colonel Koch and asked him why hadn't he been informed about what this major was doing at Third Army Headquarters. Colonel Koch told General Patton that since they had had such a bad experience with the British intelligence and signal troops attached to them in Africa and Sicily, he felt it best not to mention their presence and mission to him. General Patton took that as a reasonable and satisfactory explanation. General Patton then told me that beginning the next morning at seven I was to come to his trailer and present a short briefing on ULTRA intelligence and on what had come in over the past twenty-four hours. I was to be prepared to do that until further notice. Also, that if any single important intelligence came in, I was to get it to him or the Chief of Staff at once.[35]

These daily briefings continued until the end of the war. In the past, as Winterbotham pointed out, ULTRA was very effective; but now the impediment based on Patton's prejudices was removed, and ULTRA became much more tactically responsive. Third Army's staff quickly discarded the old Allied attitudes towards ULTRA as it discovered through Patton's new program that:

> The idea that ULTRA is useful tactically only in a static situation became ridiculous as an Army has never moved as fast and as far as the Third Army in its drive across France and ULTRA was invaluable every mile of the way . . . The operational value of the service was so impressive that General Patton never passed a special briefing. If he was unable to attend the regular meeting, he always saw to it during the day that the recipients (ULTRA officers) came over to his caravan to make their showing.[36]

One of the keys that made this information so valuable to Third Army was that Patton pushed this information down to the lowest levels. His methods sometimes went well beyond what was approved by Bletchley Park.

A letter from General Marshall that provided the governing regulations for ULTRA made some items very clear. Two of the biggest restrictions were that only "authorized recipients of ULTRA" could receive this information and "when operational action is taken on the basis of ULTRA intelligence, the utmost care must be taken, by means of proper cover, to insure that the action does not reveal or in any way suggest that this source of intelligence is at our disposal."[37] Patton and his staff pushed these two stipulations to the limit. Essentially, Marshall's instructions restricted ULTRA information from going below Army level. But from Patton's perspective, that information was needed at lower levels of command; and he used different methods that sometimes pushed or broke the rules contained in the Marshall letter. Helfers recalled one method that Patton used five or six times, which was focused on pushing information to the corps level:

> He [Patton] would come up to my map and he would ask me about a specific area. He would then ask, "Would you make me a copy on a little map of that specific area with that information on it [ULTRA]? I'm going to see General Eddy or one of the other Corps commanders because I want to discuss this with them." [With some apprehension Helfers prepared the map.] I handed it to him when he was getting into his car. I said "General Patton my instructions are that this intelligence is not to go below Army level." General Patton said "who told you that?" I said "Colonel Telford Taylor at the Embassy" [Highest Ranking American ULTRA officer in theater]. Patton said "Gimme the map. Don't worry about it, I'll assume all responsibility. I'll see that you get your map back tomorrow morning." And that's the way it worked.[38]

There is no record of how Patton presented these regulation-bending encounters, but it has become clear that many tactical actions had ULTRA influences. Even Winterbotham suspected it, as is evident in his comment: "Patton had been bound to inform General Haislip [XV Corps commander] of the source of the information."[39] But in the same story he also acknowledged that "on the whole, security was quite marvelous, considering the moves which had to be made in such a hurry."[40] Patton did not let ULTRA's influence stop at corps or even division level. Helfers also contended the general pushed this information down to one lowest tactical level of command. A small task force was responsible for the vital role of flank guard in one operation: "Colonel Harkins had a Task Force with an infantry company, artillery battery, and a tank company and they were sent out as flank guard. Well something came out of the briefing which Patton thought was something that Harkins could use. Without anything to do after the briefing, Patton said 'all right now Major . . . hot foot it over to Harkins and tell him what you just told me about that area over there.' "[41]

Patton understood the force-enhancing possibilities of ULTRA, and they had great influence on his ground scheme of maneuver. At the highest levels, ULTRA allowed the Allies to make preparations for the German counterattack at Mortain. This allowed Patton's forces to continue pouring through Avranches, which facilitated Third Army's attacks heading east, west, and south. At the lowest levels, ULTRA allowed Patton to employ economy-of-force measures effectively by giving him the exact locations, strengths, and intentions of German troops. Patton's new ULTRA system was lauded in every after-action report. The only member of Third Army headquarters who did not appreciate ULTRA's capabilities was "Willie," Patton's pit bull, who "showed his contempt for intelligence by raising his leg on one of the recipient's best maps," which caused Patton to exclaim, "you see Major what Willie thinks of your map."[42]

German Neck in a Noose
That the Allies Fail to Pull

The last 11 days of Kluge's life were spent arguing with Hitler concerning strategies associated with the Mortain area, and many of these conversations were captured by the ULTRA audience. This information proved invaluable as Patton's team planned its next move. By 1200 hours on 7 August, the German forces were brought to a standstill. At this same hour, Weyland recorded in his diary "conference with General Bradley, General Patton and General Wheeler, reference ground plans on killing German counterattack and further movements for Third Army."[43] *The Patton Papers*, which was written before ULTRA was declassified, provides some insight into this meeting. Although the book credited Patton's fine intuitive feeling for foreseeing the events of the 7th, it more importantly pointed out that "because Patton halted three divisions near the attack area . . . Bradley let him continue his sweep around the Allied right flank."[44] By this time ULTRA was also alleviating some of their fears because the Allied commanders knew that they would have ample warning that would allow them to react to any serious threats. ULTRA relieved Patton of many of his defensive duties; and after this meeting, Patton's forces were attacking the sparse German defenses to the east. These eastern drives had the potential to encircle an entire German army, but such action was dependent upon the Germans remaining infatuated with Hitler's original target—the sea at Avranches.

Indications from ULTRA remained encouraging for Patton's envelopment. It became apparent that the Germans did not to want give up on their initial plans. One Bletchley Park employee fondly reflected on this period by stating: "I can still vividly recall the exhilaration . . . in recollection they (the intercepts) surpass even D-Day for volume and importance of the information ULTRA produced. The size of the net which was being drawn round Army Group B, and the number of divisions which would be caught in it clearly depended on whether Hitler persisted with his foolhardy attack."[45]

Messages after the initial German repulse showed the enemy was willing to continue this foolhardy attack for quite some time. Unfettered by German setbacks, ULTRA revealed that the "intentions [of] 2d SS Panzer Division [were] unchanged, St. Hilaire [was] to be captured."[46] Further encouragement came on 8 August when the Seventh German Army directed an "attack by 47th Panzer Corps . . . [which was] to be continued with all forces, and the breakthrough to Avranches, decisive for the general situation, was to be achieved."[47] As the Germans remained focused on their original plan, it appeared Hitler was unaware of Army Group B's tenuous position. Every order Hitler made demanding an attack to the sea pushed the German troops' necks farther into the Allies' noose. Patton's deep drive to LeMans and the potential left turn towards Allied forces in the north presented a situation that caused General Bradley to comment, "This is an opportunity that comes to a commander not more than once in a century. We're about to destroy an entire hostile army."[48]

During this period Field Marshal Bernard L. Montgomery's forces were facing close scrutiny due to their modest gains as compared to Patton's successes in Brittany. Although Montgomery had promised to take Caen on D day (6 June 1944), he did not finish mopping up resistance until 18 July.[49] His next offensive would move at a similar sluggish pace and would hinder attempts at a greater envelopment. Most of Hitler's plans to strike Avranches were dependent upon transferring tanks from the Falaise area in order to mass his forces. During this time frame, Montgomery launched a succession of attacks focused on taking Falaise. Many ULTRA readers watched with disgust as Montgomery's forces engaged the same German troops who had movement orders to go farther into the pocket that the Allies were hoping to envelop. One such reader, Group Capt Winterbotham, made this point by stating, "Montgomery might have done better to let Eberbach's panzers go west before the Canadian attack."[50]

The manner in which the Allies were going to destroy this enveloped army remains a controversial subject. ULTRA messages showed that defenses around and south of Paris looked particularly vulnerable. Patton preferred drives farther to the east towards Chartres or Dreux before turning north for a deeper envelopment to ensure all the Germans in Normandy would be cut off, but in Patton's words "Bradley won't let me."[51] Weyland was more vocal in his objections when he was asked if he supported the early attempt to envelop the Germans at Falaise:

It just made me mad as he--. . . We were on our way. He-- we would have hit the Seine River. Then we were going to go down—my concept and then Georgie's too—hit the Seine River, cross it, of course, and then go down there and cut off that German Army which was confronting the British. But no, we got orders. As a matter of fact, General Omar Bradley came down to our headquarters and we were really rolling. We were making 30 miles a day, or something like that, and rolling along. Some opposition, nothing serious . . . So Bradley came down and said, "Well, George, starting tomorrow, I want you to do a 90-degree crossover turn and head due north instead of Paris." Well Georgie was amazed. I was amazed . . . Well, I threw my tin hat on the ground. I said "My God, this is a piecemeal meddle." I said "We're ruined. We'll be at the Seine River. The Redball Express can still support them there." I hadn't even started using the troop carriers to support us . . . "We're on the go" I said. "Boy, General Bradley, why don't you

59

just let us keep going? There's nothing of any consequence to stop us. Well, the Germans troops are massed to our north, and we're south of them, and moving. We'll get in behind them. What's wrong with that?" He kind of smiled and said, "Well you've got a point, and it's probably a good one, but this is the way it's going to be done."[52]

Patton and Weyland complied with these orders, and on 8 August Third Army gave the directive to "advance on the [northward] axis [of] LeMans–Alencon–Sees to prepare for further action against [the] enemy flank and rear."[53] The following day an ULTRA message revealed that the Germans did not anticipate this northward advance, and they acknowledged Patton's exceptional employment of intelligence in the following message: "Allied movements and behavior lead to [the] conclusion that [the] Allies very thoroughly informed on [the] German situation and state of forces. Jagdkorps [is] not repeat not expecting [the] Allies to wheel northwards but rather continue [their] main thrust to [the] east and southeast."[54] This was encouraging, for Patton's forces were now driving north; but the best confirmation that Germans were susceptible to an envelopment came on 10 August.

Once again Hitler's prose came through ULTRA, and he left very little to Kluge's imagination for this attack. Hitler had apparently not lost his preference for Avranches and the sea:

> Attack on southern wing of Seventh Army will be conducted by Panzer Gruppe Eberbach after regrouping and bringing up of decisive offensive arms. On its success depends the fate of the battle of France. "I order" command of attack, General Eberbach to whom a newly formed Fuehrungsstab is being brought up with Oberstleutnant Von Kluge [Field Marshal's son] as Chief of staff . . . Objective of the attack, the sea at Avranches to which a bold and unhesitating thrust through is to be made. Rear attacking waves swinging north as opportunity occurs . . . Time of attack, probably on eleventh. Be prepared for a postponement at short notice of 12 to 24 hours.[55]

Hitler's message assured Patton that the Germans' attention was diverted away from his forces thrusting north.

ULTRA provided more encouraging news from the tactical levels. Reports among the various units displayed the disorganization that existed within the German lines. One message stated, "Lack of clear knowledge on the location of his own troops and [the] undisciplined withdrawal even before slight Allied pressure make it appear possible that [the] commander of the regiment on the left operating on the Corps boundary is not in control of his troops."[56] That same day, ULTRA provided a rest and refit message that reduced the number of German fighter groups from 17 to 13.[57] This reduction helped create an environment in which Patton's air-ground team could thrive, and it wasted no time heading north towards its next objective at Alencon.

During the operations around Alencon, Third Army and XIX TAC demonstrated the complementary nature of air-ground operations. Some efforts involved tactical expedients, as illustrated by the following example: "enemy tanks were holding up an American column, fifteen 500-pounders were dropped and . . . the US column was seen to move forward."[58] Other air efforts required more detailed planning and coordination. Patton wanted the ground forces to advance on their objectives as quickly as possible in order to exploit the German's attention to the west at Avranches. Airpower facilitated these attacks. The speed of Patton's maneuver to Alencon surprised Montgomery, whose action in contrast to Patton's, according to Russell F. Weigley "appears to have bogged itself in timidity and succumbed to the legendary vice of over caution."[59] Third Army's next target was Argentan. This city and those beyond it would be greatly affected by Montgomery's cautious nature because Argentan was eight miles beyond Bradley's army group boundary.

While Patton was moving north, Kluge and Hitler continued to debate the future of France. Hitler was still focused on Avranches, but Kluge was able to promote a secondary strike against Patton's forces to the south. This information did not escape Third Army headquarters, and Martin Blumenson summed up Patton's thoughts in the following observation:

> With ULTRA intercepts warning Allied commanders of a German strike against Haislip's (Patton's XV Corps Commander) flanks, was it wise to let Haislip go ahead? Or was it better to hold him where he was and let him assume a defensive posture? As always, Patton opted for audacity, letting Haislip close the pocket. If that course increased the risks, so be it. On the other hand, perhaps the Germans would never be able to attack Haislip's flank. Even if they did, they lacked the strength, Patton surmised, to create more than a fleeting crisis. Either way, the Allies seemed about to eliminate the two German armies west of the

Seine River. That goal, firmly, in Patton's mind, warranted accepting danger.[60]

ULTRA probably contributed to Patton's audacity. Numerous ULTRA messages reported that units inside the Falaise pocket informed higher headquarters that they were short of gasoline, ammunition, and transportation, and that heavy losses meant that some units existed in name only. Gen Wade H. Haislip's ground activity proved many of these reports to be true. His troops initially found Argentan defended by a German bakery company.[61] Patton knew the Germans would not stay in the western portion of the Falaise pocket forever. Whether the German forces were withdrawing from the pocket or attempting to counter the Third Army drive from the south, Patton knew he was in a foot race with the Germans to secure the rear areas. Any delays would ensure that the Germans would replace bakery companies with panzer divisions. Therefore, Patton stretched his authority when he ordered XV Corps "upon capture of Argentan push on slowly in the direction of Falaise . . . [then] continue to push on slowly until you contact our Allies."[62]

This movement went well beyond Twelfth Army Group's boundary, and Patton was obliged immediately to inform Bradley of this action. Bradley told Patton to stop offensive operations. His decision has been the source of controversy ever since. Unfortunately for Patton, Eisenhower would not take control of ground operations until 1 September 1944; this left Montgomery as the de facto European theater of operations ground force commander, even though Bradley was commanding the army group. Bradley's response was probably influenced by events that occurred earlier that day at Montgomery's headquarters. When the news reached Montgomery of Haislip's progress beyond Argentan, he turned to his chief of staff, Francis De Guingand, and ordered him to "tell Bradley they ought to get back."[63] This order clearly agitated De Guingand, which led him to comment to Montgomery's G-2 that "Monty is too tidy."[64]

Patton spent most of 13 August calling headquarters trying to overturn the order. ULTRA assured Third Army that Hitler's interest was still focused on Avranches; and the German counterattack on his flank, as expected, was not materializing in great strength. Early that morning, Leven Allen (Bradley's chief of staff), confirmed Bradley's stop order. Patton pleaded with Allen to convince Bradley to talk to Montgomery for him. Bradley's G-3 eventually made the call to Montgomery's headquarters, requesting permission to drive north of Argentan. Unfortunately, De Guingand's answer was "I am sorry." De Guingand revealed in his memoirs his belief "in the ability of the Americans to have gone beyond Argentan and to have closed the pocket. The blame for the failure to do so fell on Montgomery. The Americans regarded the army group boundary as a firm restriction against further movement. They needed Montgomery's invitation to cross, and Montgomery should have erased the line on the map and let them proceed."[65]

Montgomery's halt order remained in effect until the British and Canadians captured Falaise, which did not occur until 16 August. In the interim XIX TAC attempted to make up for the stationary Third Army ground forces that were awaiting the British successes in the north. On 13 August, 37 P-47 pilots found 800–1,000 motor vehicles of all descriptions west of Argentan. The flight pounced on the column destroying 400–500 vehicles, with one pilot in the attack employing his belly tank on 12 trucks—which resulted in an explosion that left all of them on fire.[66] The following day's events further confirmed Patton's suspicions that the enemy was extremely vulnerable. At 1100 hours XIX TAC's 511th Squadron reported northeast of Argentan "the phenomenon of ground troops surrendering to air," and fighter command provided the location of the 300–400 white flag waving troops to the closest "unemployed" units still held up by Montgomery's stop order.[67]

Patton was livid as Haislip's forces idly waited for the British to close the gap. By the 14th, the Germans clearly understood their dire circumstances. At midday, the German Seventh Army "requested to withdraw [the] front [of] Seventh Army and [the] left wing [of] Panzer Army Five under the protection of Panzer Gruppe Eberbach to the line Falaise–Argentan."[68] Patton knew his opportunity to close the Falaise Gap was becoming increasingly fleeting because the longer Third Army waited, the more its northern route would be populated with escaping German forces from the west. ULTRA provided an excellent summary of the German withdrawal. Patton monitored the Germans' exploitation of Montgomery's mistake, and his frustration erupted at Helfers during a briefing when he declared, "If Montgomery does not get a move on I'm going to drive those Germans right up his a--!"[69] A calmer Patton reflected in his diary, "I believe that order . . . emanated from 21st Army Group, and was either due to [British] jealousy of the Americans or to utter ignorance of the situation or a combination of the two."[70]

When the Canadians finally took Falaise on the 16th, Montgomery found a situation significantly different from the night of the 12th. Haislip's 90th Division was heavily engaged with German troops desperately trying to keep the gap open. On the 17th Patton created a provisional corps (2d French Armor Division, 90th Infantry Division, and 80th Infantry Division) under his chief of staff, Gen Hugh J. Gaffey, to implement the order to close the gap.[71] By this time the Falaise Gap was a lost opportunity. A desperate, cornered enemy now inhabited an area that was once devoid of German forces. XV Corps was denied the previous advantages of Mortain. As opposed to rapidly capturing rear-area towns and setting up defensive positions that were easily supported by air, Gaffey's southern corps and Montgomery's forces from the north had to endure hard fighting, which finally closed the gap on 20 August. The Allied ground scheme of maneuver was denied the crushing victory once promised to it, but it did complement the air attacks that significantly helped with the defeat of German forces caught in the pocket.

Airpower's systematic reduction of enemy forces left a strong impression on the Germans caught within the pocket. Gen Fritz Bayerlein, commander, Kampfgruppe Panzer Lehr, provided some insight into what it was like to be on the receiving end of the Falaise air attack when he said,

> Traffic was in a terrific snarl in the village, moving north and east to get out of the Falaise–Argentan trap . . . Punctually at 0900 in the morning of the 13th came the fighter-bombers. They swept in very low over at least 250 motor transport, trucks, cannon, and nebelwerfer on the roads in and around the village and nearby fields and orchards. They hit a truck train of rocket ammunition right off the bat, and this

started exploding and throwing rockets in all directions. The streets of the town were so littered with the burning remains of trucks and equipment as to be impassable, yet the fighters kept on until it was practically dark, after which two-motor bombers came in and bombed intermittently at night.[72]

By 17 August the German escape attempts were in full swing. Targets were so numerous that the Allies had very little trouble finding use for their ordnance, and XIX TAC rapidly massed its forces to capitalize on the opportunities the Germans afforded them. Not even weather protected the enemy: "The Germans tried another mass movement out of the pocket. They figured that low clouds were a reasonably good safeguard against our aircraft, and they began to take to the roads two and three abreast in anything that had wheels. A short squadron of American fighter-bombers dived dangerously low through the clouds and saw the traffic jam. They sent word back to headquarters, and soon the sky was so full of British and American fighter-bombers that they had to form queues to make their bomb runs. The gigantic offensive kept up until after nightfall."[73] The Germans continually acknowledged the effects of Allied airpower. Many were impressed with road attacks and claimed fighters would "pounce down even on a single vehicle or motor cyclist," while another officer summarized the frustrations of many POWs when he said, "you have bombed and strafed all the roads causing complete congestion and heavy traffic jams. You have destroyed most of our petrol and oil dumps, so there is no future in continuing to fight."[74]

Although XIX TAC's operations may have been very successful in Falaise, they too were not above British interference denying them more effective results on the battlefield. The morning of the 18th found a sight that had become routine during the Falaise Gap operations. P-47s found 1,000–1,500 vehicles parked bumper to bumper in the Argentan–Trun area. Further reconnaissance revealed 1,000 more, and the standard call back to higher headquarters was made to share the wealth. To the disappointment of the XIX TAC pilots, they received an order similar to their ground counterparts, which was "do not attack because they were outside of their responsibility."[75] The majority of the targets were in the British sector; and as opposed to queuing as they did before, the British wanted sole propriety of this 7,000-vehicle target. Although the British would damage or destroy almost 3,000 vehicles, the XIX TAC was upset that this "stop order" would deny them "a chance at the big jackpot."[76]

Stop orders—whether directed at ground or air forces—can be debated long after a conflict has ended, but they represent some of the difficulties that are inherent in coalition warfare. Montgomery's delays allowed the Germans to recover personnel, panzers, and field guns that became the cadre of divisions that helped carry on the European campaign. But coalition warfare by its nature breeds different solutions for different problems. Although the Normandy campaign cost the Germans 250,000 casualties and overwhelming amounts of equipment, Patton's forces saw the Falaise Gap as an opportunity lost because for the majority of the campaign, they could only hit the fleeing Germans with their air arm.[77] This would not be the last time Patton had a difference of opinion with Montgomery's tactics, but in this case Patton employed other Third Army assets and focused them on Patton's original goal—the Seine River.

During the Mortain and the Falaise Gap battles, ULTRA and airpower afforded Patton many force-enhancing capabilities that allowed him to prosecute his campaign effectively. During the Mortain counterattack, Patton used his employment of three divisions as a backstop for First Army as justification to convince Bradley to allow him to press his attacks to the east. Mortain also became the genesis for an upgraded ULTRA program that helped tighten his decision cycle and push vital information to lower echelons of command. Airpower during this campaign continued to refine its transition from attacking static targets with First Army into a cavalry-type organization that could break free a stalled tank column with a single pass of fifteen 500-pound bombs. While Third Army was halted, ground units became supporting elements to the XIX TAC. Third Army rounded up prisoners and held defensive positions as Weyland hit the Falaise Gap with the only weapons that were permitted by higher headquarters. ULTRA also benefited from Patton's rapid advances. Desperate, retreating Germans generated increased radio traffic that provided Patton clear insight into all facets of the Germans' capabilities and intentions.

This phase clearly displayed the potential synergy of ULTRA, airpower, and ground scheme of maneuver; but it also demonstrated the adverse effects on this synergy when one of the elements was denied. During the Mortain counteroffensive, all elements (ULTRA, airpower, and ground scheme of maneuver) contributed to produce overwhelming results that destroyed the German attack. In contrast, the Falaise Gap failed to yield the same conclusive results. Higher headquarters denied Patton his ground scheme of maneuver, and he attempted to strike the enemy with his remaining two force enhancers. ULTRA-informed airpower destroyed enemy troops and equipment; but towards the end of the campaign, British air efforts also denied the XIX TAC the ability to fully apply its destructive power. Eventually, higher headquarters lifted their restrictions on Patton's force-enhancing trinity; but by this time the window of opportunity had closed. The vulnerable German troops that were pushing their necks farther into the Allies' noose became aware of their precarious position and were no longer in danger of a Falaise envelopment. This fact did not deter Patton as he employed his force-enhancing troika towards his original target area for an envelopment—the Seine River.

Notes

1. Great Britain Public Record Office, "ULTRA: Main Series of Signals Conveying Intelligence," Bletchley Park, 1944, reel 34, XL 4917. Copy located in Auburn University Library, Auburn, Ala.

2. Ibid.

3. Ibid., XL 4991.

4. Ibid., XL 4997.

5. Ibid., XL 4999.

6. Melvin C. Helfers, Personal Papers—"My Personal Experience with High Level Intelligence" (Charleston, S.C.: The Citadel Archives, November 1974), 7.

7. Melvin C. Helfers, video tape interview at The Citadel (Charleston, S.C.: The Citadel Archives, 2 October 1984).

8. Helfers, Personal Papers, 9.

9. Oscar W. Koch and Robert G. Hays, *G-2: Intelligence for Patton* (Philadelphia: Whitmore Publishing, 1971), 64.

10. Helfers, Personal Papers, 8.

11. Ibid.

12. Martin Blumenson, *The Patton Papers,* vol. 2, *1940–1945* (Boston: Houghton Mifflin, 1974), 503.

13. Melvin C. Helfers, video tape interview at The Citadel (Charleston, S.C.: The Citadel Archives, 9 October 1984).

14. Great Britain Public Record Office, reel 34, XL 5027.

15. Ibid., XL 5053.

16. O. P. Weyland, Report 168.7104-1—"Weyland Diary—XIX TAC" (Albert F. Simpson Historical Research Center: Weyland Collection, 18 May 1945), diary for 6 August 1944, entry 1930.

17. Ibid., 6 August 1944, entry 2300.

18. "Weyland Diary—XIX TAC," 7 August 1944, entry 0830.

19. Koch and Hays, 65.

20. David Irving, *Hitler's War* (New York: Viking Press, 1977), 684–85.

21. XIX TAC Staff, Report 168.7104-64—"Twelve Thousand Fighter-Bomber Sorties" (Albert F. Simpson Historical Research Center: Weyland Collection, 30 September 1944), 8.

22. Ibid., 9.

23. Office of the Assistant Chief of Air Staff for Intelligence, Report 168.7104-92—"IMPACT—US Tactical Air Power in Europe" (Albert F. Simpson Historical Research Center: Weyland Collection, May 1945), 28.

24. Seymour Freidin, Werner Kreipe, and William Richardson, eds., *The Fatal Decisions* (New York: W. Sloan Associates, 1956), 224.

25. Ronald Lewin, *ULTRA Goes to War: The First Account of World War II's Greatest Secret Based on Official Documents* (London: Hutchinson Co., 1978), 339.

26. Ibid.

27. Warrack Wallace, SRH-108—"Report on Assignment with the Third United States Army, 15 August–18 September 1944" (National Archives: Record Group 457, 21 May 1945), 3.

28. Lewin, 339.

29. Irving, 684.

30. Ibid., 689.

31. Freidin, Kreipe, and Richardson, 227.

32. F. W. Winterbotham, *The ULTRA Secret* (New York: Harper & Row, 1974), 160.

33. George C. Marshall, SRH-026—"Marshall Letter to Eisenhower on the Use of ULTRA Intelligence" (National Archives: Record Group 457, 15 March 1944), 2.

34. Helfers, Personal Papers, 3–4

35. Ibid., 8.

36. Wallace, 4–5.

37. Marshall.

38. Melvin C. Helfers, video tape interview at The Citadel (Charleston, S.C.: The Citadel Archives, 16 October 1984).

39. Winterbotham, 219.

40. Ibid.

41. Helfers, video tape interview, 16 October 1984.

42. Ibid.; and Wallace, 5.

43. "Weyland Diary—XIX TAC," 7 August 1944, entry 1200.

44. Blumenson, 503.

45. Ralph Bennett, *ULTRA in the West: The Normandy Campaign, 1944–45* (New York: Scribner, 1980), 118.

46. Great Britain Public Record Office, reel 35, XL 5119.

47. Ibid., reel 34, XL 5248.

48. Omar N. Bradley, *A Soldier's Story* (New York: Henry Holt Co., 1951), 375.

49. Thomas Parrish, *The American Codebreakers—The US Role in ULTRA* (Chelsea, Mich.: Scarborough Press, 1991), 213–14.

50. Winterbotham, 154.

51. Blumenson, 504.

52. Ralph Stephenson, Report K239.0512-813—"Interview with General O. P. Weyland" (Air Force Historical Research Center: Weyland Collection, 19 November 1974), 89–91.

53. Third US Army, "After Action Report, 1 Aug 44–9 May 45," vol. 1, Annex N, Third US Army Directives, Regensburg, Germany, 1945, IV. Copy located in Auburn University Library, Auburn, Ala.

54. Great Britain Public Record Office, reel 35, XL 5356.

55. Ibid., XL 5461.

56. Ibid., XL 5476.

57. Ibid., XL 5521.

58. XIX TAC Staff, Report 168.7104-64—"Twelve Thousand Fighter-Bomber Sorties," 16.

59. Martin Blumenson, *The Battle of the Generals: The Untold Story of the Falaise Pocket* (New York: W. Morrow, 1993), 205–6.

60. Ibid., 207.

61. Ibid., 205.

62. Third US Army, "After Action Report," Annex N, Third US Army Directives, V.

63. Blumenson, *The Battle of the Generals*, 208.

64. Ibid.

65. Ibid., 209–10.

66. XIX TAC Staff, Report 168.7104-64—"Twelve Thousand Fighter-Bomber Sorties," 17.

67. Ibid., 18.

68. Great Britain Public Record Office, reel 36, XL 6312.

69. Helfers, video tape interview, 16 October 1984.

70. Blumenson, *The Patton Papers*, 508–9.

71. Third US Army, "After Action Report," Annex N, Third US Army Directives, VII.

72. Willis Thornton, Report 168.7104-95—"Interrogation of General Fritz Bayerlein" (Albert F. Simpson Historical Research Center: Weyland Collection, 29 May 1945), 9.

73. XIX TAC Staff, Report 168.7104-81—"Planes over Patton" (Albert F. Simpson Historical Research Center: Weyland Collection, 30 October 1944), 27.

74. Gerry B. Jepson, Report 533.4501-9—"Assessments of Air Attacks as Determined from Prisoners of War" (Albert F. Simpson Historical Research Center: Aerospace Studies Institute, 18 August 1944), 1–2.

75. XIX TAC Staff, Report 168.7104-64—"Twelve Thousand Fighter-Bomber Sorties," 24.

76. Ibid.

77. Lewin, 345.

Chapter 5

Tale of Two Rivers—Seine and Loire

*To attack with limited forces I have now left available—
since I occupy a 300 mile front—I'm taking chances, but I
am convinced that the situation in the German Army warrants the taking of such risks.*

—George S. Patton Jr.

*He [Patton] got enough information from ULTRA to know
there was no danger from his southern flank across Loire
River, it was unheard of that an army would drive through
enemy territory without flank guard. That was where the
19th TAC came in and the Air Force was his flank guard.*

—Melvin C. Helfers

Based on his experiences in World War I and his various
European tours, Patton had very specific ideas for his upcoming assault on northern Europe. This was to be Patton's third
trip across France, and he made his desired route very clear
to his staff. Colonel Koch arrived at Knutsford, England, on 23
March 1944; and in his first meeting with Patton since Sicily,
Koch found his old boss in a customary position—bent over a
map table. Patton declared "Koch, I want all your G-2 planning
directed here [Metz, France]," Patton then swept his finger
starting at Nantes on the Atlantic Coast, along the Loire River
eastward, and noted "I do not intend to go south of the Loire
unless it is necessary to avoid a right angle turn."[1] Koch immediately realized the importance of this meeting, and he later
reflected "In the broadest terms, Patton had just stated his
EEI's [essential elements of information] for the planned Third
Army offensive on the European continent . . . The task facing
my intelligence staff was now clear. Anything which might affect the Third Army mission, from that coast of France all the
way to Metz by way of a circuitous route through Brittany, was

now of critical concern."[2] Patton's original concept was sound. It appeared from all indications resonating from the enemy that an eastward drive along the Loire by way of Metz could deliver Patton's forces to the German border in relatively little time. Unfortunately, the German dispositions and intentions that Koch was tracking were not the biggest hazards to the Third Army's mission. Patton correctly identified the real threat when he wrote, "My only worries are my relations, not my enemies."[3]

Patton's Original Plan Pursued.

Patton's swift drive to LeMans showed that there was great disorganization within the German ranks and that the only way to nurture this confusion was to grant them no reprieve from attack. General Bradley's order to drive northwards towards Alencon upset Patton and Weyland because they felt this pocket was too shallow and their bigger prize was at the Seine River. Contrary to legend, Patton always followed orders; but he also had the habit of suggesting alternative strategies while implementing orders with which he may not have agreed. This clearly was the case when Bradley's northern drive to Falaise turned into Montgomery's halt at Argentan.

Third Army's breakout and exploitation in early August shocked the Germans, and ULTRA captured their panic as the Germans struggled to prepare defensive lines. A message of 10 August 1944 displayed the situation within the German lines that may explain Patton and Weyland's objections to the shallow attempt at an envelopment or the more ill-planned stop order. The ULTRA intercept was a directive from *Oberkommando der Wehrmacht (OKW)* to the military commander of France that stated,

> OKW orders rearward positions along the Marne [River]. The military control of the development of a special ops [operations] staff to be set up with Military Commander France. Personnel to be employed— Fortress Construction Battalions. In addition, French population [is] to be employed on a large scale, severest measures [are to be used] to put sufficient numbers rapidly to work. Three blocking preparations to be pushed forward with [the] greatest of emphasis . . . Preparations to enroll civilians on [the] largest scale to be based on commune lists of

inhabitants from 16 to 60 years old . . . Inhabitants [are] to supply en-
trenching tools.[4]

These positions were behind the Seine River, and the next day
the ULTRA audience received further confirmation that the
Germans had little current capability to defend west of the
Seine. A message from 11 August ordered a commission to ensure "arrangements [are] made for [the] evacuation in [the]
areas of Melun, Paris, Chartres and [the] north[ern] part of
Orleans."[5] The situation was clear to Weyland, as he indicated
in his diary on 13 August: "G-2-3 Meeting—[showed] All reports, ground and air, indicate withdrawal of Germans to [the]
east."[6] The following day, numerous ULTRA messages would
provide Patton's road map to further exploit the German gaps
in the east.

At 0218 hours on the 14th, ULTRA provided Patton encouraging news for future operations when it reported the Germans'
appreciation of his southern forces near LeMans. This situation
report stated, "To be assumed that Allies, [are] bringing up further forces to [the] area [of] LeMans, [they] will continue [to]
thrust northward in [the] general direction [of] Rouen (a city on
the Seine). Covering lines envisaged were for the time being no
longer effective."[7] Later in the day, an additional message provided the specific weak points in the German lines. The following message indicates how German higher headquarters franti-
cally tried to plug holes in their defenses.

> [Request] Up to one Army into [the] area south of Paris by quickest
> possible means . . . 64th Infantry not to be brought up to 19th Army,
> but [instead] to [an] area southeast [of] Paris. Luftflotte 3 [is] to subor-
> dinate 1000 men to [the] army for ground fighting in area south [of]
> Paris–Dreux–Chateaudun–Orleans–Montaris . . . 15th Army, without
> awaiting arrival of static divisions, [is instructed] to pull out [the] 1st
> and then 2nd Infantry Divisions and [are to] send them by quickest
> possible means to [the] area south of Paris. Some of the above meas-
> ures are being carried out in that [the] 6th Parachute Division is to
> move into [an] area around Chartres.[8]

Patton knew he was in a footrace with the German forces
and could not stand still when undefended territory beckoned
to the east. Patton also knew that in this scenario, time was
against him; and within 24 hours of Montgomery's stop order,
Patton had managed to get his forces moving again. On this

same day, Patton devised a plan that divided XV Corps into two entities. The first half would comply with the Argentan stop order and assume defensive positions, while the other half would complement a larger force that was tasked to exploit the German situation in the east. After consulting General Haislip on the plan, Patton—the politician—went to higher headquarters to win approval for his latest concept. A secret to his success lay in the following diary entry: "I then flew back to see Bradley and sell him the plan. He consented, and even permitted me to change it so as to move XX Corps on Chartres, the XV Corps on Dreux, and XII Corps on Orleans . . . It is really a great plan, wholly my own, and I made Bradley think he thought of it. Oh, what a tangled web we weave when we first practice to deceive. I am very happy and elated. I got all the Corps moving by 2030, so that if Monty tries to be careful it will be too late."[9] ULTRA provided a road map to the Seine, and Patton knew he had a small window of opportunity. In order to beat the Germans to the punch, Patton would require every advantage that ULTRA and airpower could provide.

One of the first units that Patton got moving at 2030 hours on the 14th was XII Corps. It was concentrated southeast of LeMans awaiting orders, and Patton directed it to proceed directly to Orleans. Patton noted XII Corps's initial drive from LeMans as a model of air-ground cooperation, and he provided insight into his combinations with the following passage:

> Just east of Le Mans was one of the best examples of armor and air cooperation I have ever seen. For about two miles the road was full of enemy motor transport and armor, many of which bore the unmistakable calling card of a P-47 fighter-bomber—namely a group of .50-caliber holes. Whenever armor and air can work together in this way, the results are sure to be excellent. Armor can move fast enough to prevent the enemy having time to deploy off the roads, and so long as he stays on the roads the fighter-bomber is one of the most deadly opponents. To accomplish this happy teamwork two things are necessary: first, intimate confidence and friendship between air and ground; second, incessant and apparently ruthless driving on the part of the ground commander.[10]

Patton's air-ground team made excellent time; and by the night of the 15th, XII Corps confirmed the German evacuation order that was identified in ULTRA. Patton's forces found the large airport in Orleans, which had been strongly fortified with antiaircraft and antitank guns, virtually undefended. After capturing the airport, XII Corps finished the job the following morning with a two-pronged attack that crushed the slight opposition that still existed within the city.[11]

On 14 August Patton's two other initial targets (Chartres and Dreux) also showed encouraging signs for Third Army's selected routes of advance. Air reconnaissance summaries from XIX TAC stated that the "pilots reported fires at Chartres airfield, which appear[ed] unserviceable, and a violent explosion at the Dreux airdrome . . . [that made it appear that] the Luftwaffe was pulling out."[12] ULTRA information was further confirmed when XV Corps met "only a few lightly defended road blocks"; and when they surrounded Dreux, XV Corps only had to "fire at some German troops fleeing eastward" in order to capture the town.[13] During this drive time was critical; and XIX TAC also ensured that piecemeal German units would not slow Patton's forces as the following report indicated. "North of Dreux, eight P-47s flying armored column cover were vectored by the 5th Armored Division to a road junction where anti-tank guns and infantry were holding up the advance . . . Our Thunderbolts attacked it with six 500-pound bombs, four frag clusters, and strafing. Results were not observed, but the ground forces indicated that the guns were destroyed, and they congratulated the squadron leader."[14]

Complementing the obvious contributions from the air, ULTRA appears to have also greatly influenced this campaign. Bennett recalled "unprecedented amounts of Enigma traffic were being intercepted, and most of it was decoded with such rapidity that signal after signal could be prepared so close to the German time of origin, that each seemed more urgent than the last."[15] During this period Helfers remembered the importance and Patton's rapid assimilation of this information: "I remember one time he [Patton] called me in one afternoon, [he] asked me a few questions and looked at my map." After it was all over with, he said "Thank you very much Major, you have saved me the service of two divisions."[16] In this scenario Patton could neither waste time in needless battles nor waste troops on unnecessary flank missions. Patton knew the locations of the enemy defenses, and he maneuvered his forces around the impediments to ensure that he beat the Germans to the undefended positions in the rear. Unfortunately for the commanders not indoctrinated to ULTRA commanders, some of these movements may have appeared haphazard with no great purpose. One example of lower-level frustration with higher headquarters' taskings came from the official US Army History of World War II:

> General Irwin [Commander of 5th Division, XV Corps] who was less than fully informed on the big picture, [claimed that] "sudden and unexpected changes cause[d] considerable confusion in arrangements, transportation and plans," particularly since there was "no indication of reasons for orders." His bewilderment increased during the next few days when "orders made no sense at all" and prompted "great confusion." Between 12 and 16 August, Irwin received conflicting orders that indicated not much more than changing directions of march. Strained communications, sketchy information, and a surprising absence of German opposition characterized his division's movements. (Emphasis added)[17]

Although the Third Army forces that attacked Chartres encountered the most resistance, they still cited the "excellent road net and sparseness of the enemy" as the reasons for the successful drive to their objective.[18] Patton's troops were successfully employing his style of warfare, and the Third Army's initial objectives had been captured in their entirety by 16 August 1944 (map 5).

Contrary to the wishes of many Parisians, Patton's next objective was the Seine River to facilitate a second envelopment north of the French capital. Although XV Corps's eastward drive placed it only 37 miles from Paris, Patton knew a Seine River crossing there would destroy his race to the German undefended rear. Patton found much more advantageous crossing points north of the city that involved less fanfare and resistance. This northward drive would also resemble Patton and Weyland's original plan. This thrust could provide an opportunity to catch the Germans who escaped the Falaise Gap and also push the German river-crossing points farther down the Seine where the river was wider and more difficult to cross.[19]

The Germans' appreciation for the ongoing race to the Seine was not lost in ULTRA messages. One situation report stated "a

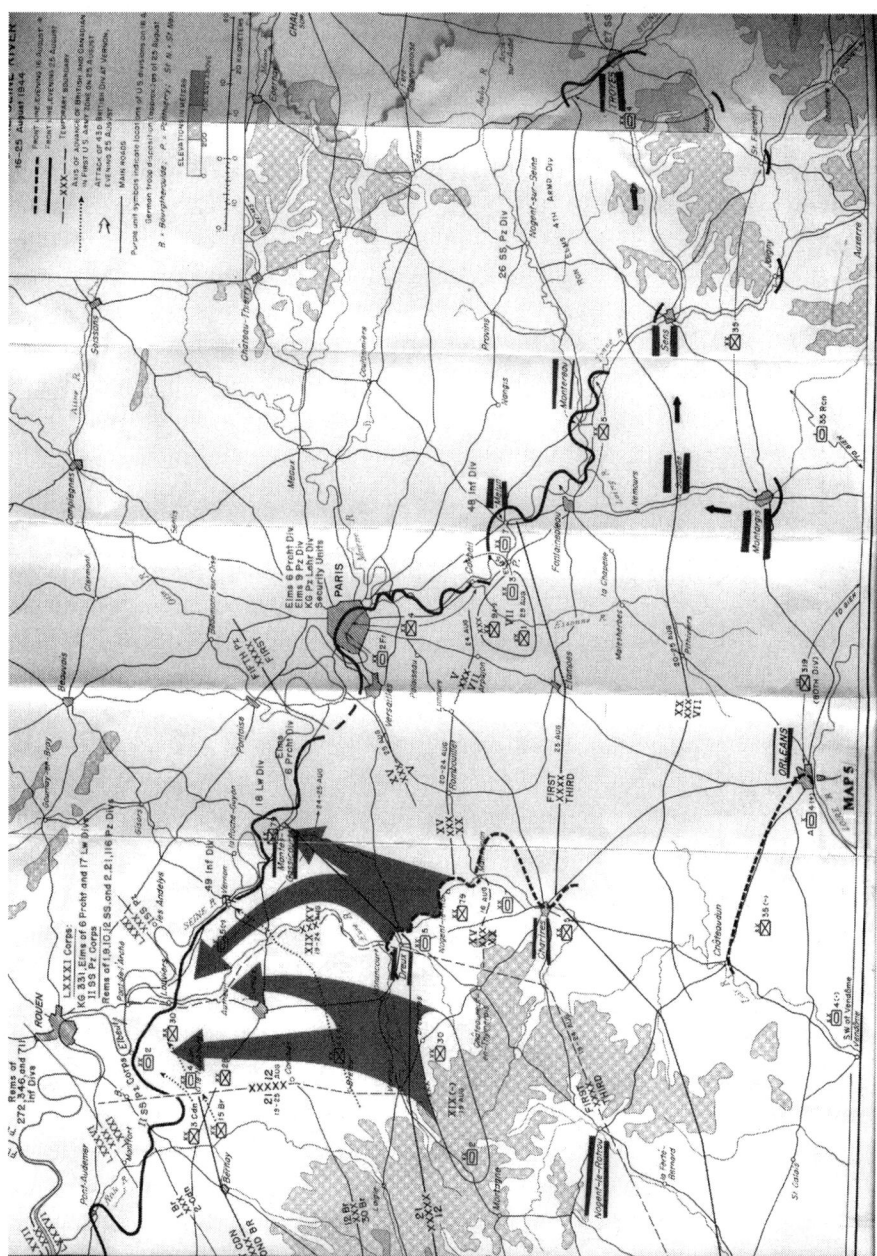

Map 5. Drive to the Seine River

new factor is that the 7th American Armored Division is attacking through Nogent. Situation at [the] bottleneck [is] still such that a certain degree of orderly evacuation is possible. If there is any hesitation, development of [the] situation [for the] Army Group cannot be foreseen.[20] Although the Germans understood the importance of beating Patton to the rear, their intentions exceeded their capabilities. Numerous ULTRA reports showed why there would be hesitations. "Situation [on] both sides [of] Falaise [is] apparently extremely serious. Resistance of the troops, weakened to utmost as regards [to] both personnel and material, not far from collapse. Consequences incalculable. Despite redoubled Allied air effort, which was intolerable for the troops, five heavy flak batteries have been made available exclusively for A/T [anti-tank] defense on north front . . . Request that bringing up ammunition be increased maximum possible."[21] Ammunition was not the only shortage the Germans were enduring, as another ULTRA intercept stated "fuel situation [is] so strained that supply journeys and removal of wounded in part stopped."[22] Patton refused to let the Germans rectify their situation as his attention focused on the most expeditious route across the Seine.

In order to conserve Allied gas and supplies, Patton gave priority to XV Corps and directed it to "move early 18 August to secure a position in the vicinity of Mantes–Gassicourt to interdict [the] Seine River."[23] Earlier that morning (0044 hours), ULTRA showed that this route of advance would be an excellent crossing point. In this message the German 352d Division was instructed that they were "under orders to withdraw in [the] face of Allied pressure to Seine crossing at Mantes and Melun."[24] Unfortunately, XX Corps was not ordered to attack Melun until 20 August; and it found defensive forces waiting. But XV Corps had a relatively easy drive to Mantes. It quickly crushed the assortment of German stragglers that were placed at roadblocks, and the following day XV Corps found Mantes–Gassicourt abandoned.[25]

The easy capture of Mantes also revealed that there was nothing preventing a Seine crossing at this location; therefore, XV Corps crossed the river and awaited further orders. This action across the Seine did not win Patton the praise one might expect as his aide-de-camp's notes indicate.

We had just finished pushing up to and against the Seine River at Mantes–Gassicourt; returned to our headquarters and on our arrival were informed by the Chief of Staff that Gen. B[radley] was on his way and was "fit to be tied." He wanted to see Gen. P[atton] . . . General B. arrived and he immediately launched into the fact that they had had a big conference and decided that Third Army shouldn't go beyond Druex and Chartres . . . [and towards] the Seine [so as to] leave an escape route for the Germans in the Falaise pocket. After Gen. B. had informed Gen. P. [he] was not to advance any farther and that was that. Gen. P. told Gen. B. that since he was already to the Seine River, in fact had pi--ed in the river that morning and had just come back from there, what would he want him to do—pull back? After much discussion Gen. B. told him how strong the people [Germans] were in the Falaise pocket and he didn't think Gen. P. would be able to contain them, and it was his orders to leave an escape route to the east [for them]. General P. asked him if he ever knew him to give up a piece of ground he had taken. Gen. B. said, "No, but this is different." Gen. P. said that he could and would hold it, if Gen. B. would agree. So it was agreed that he would hold what he had, which we did, thereby closing the escape that they had been wanting to hold open. Gen. B. left Gen. P.'s headquarters quite cheerfully, after saying to Gen. P., "It certainly is a pleasure to talk to someone who is sure and confident. The picture looks much different from here. But for my sake stay put there now— don't advance any farther across the river. I'll try to sell them this but . . .," etc.[26]

The notes from this encounter ended with Patton's aide commenting "without this crossing of the Seine . . . Montgomery might well still be sitting on his Caen."[27] This statement expressed the frustrations that Patton and his staff had with the overly cautious nature of the British and their influence on Bradley and, later, Eisenhower. Daily ULTRA intercepts showed that the German army was no longer composed of the unbeatable "supermen" that had shocked the European continent earlier in the war. Mortain proved that ULTRA and airpower could identify and destroy large attack formations, but some could not transition to this new phase of the war. Unfortunately, cautious advances allowed the Germans to set up defenses in any threatened area. By the time the lethargic forces capitalized on these attacks, another determined battle would ensue, causing numerous additional casualties and slower progression. Patton realized this and implemented a campaign focused on speed. He did this to avoid the slow-going hedgerow fighting of June and July. In August 1944 Patton's rapid, low-cost drives proved that cautious attacks were actually more dangerous, and he made this very clear in the following comment that summarized his strategy in France: "Whenever you slow anything down, you waste human lives. Up to the present, we traded about between 10 to 12 [Germans] for 1 [American] . . . The last war was a slow one, one with a narrow front, very great depth. In this war, there is no front. There is very little depth . . . [In this war] we cut through and wipe them out. If we hit opposition, we try not to boot it out. We try to hold and go around and then have the infantry clean it out."[28] Patton eventually talked Bradley into letting the XV Corps push the attack north along the banks of the Seine for a second envelopment. It took two days for XV Corps to start moving because once again, Montgomery had reservations about the Americans crossing army boundary group lines into the British sector.[29] The delay gave the Germans time to construct defensive positions and take advantage of the terrain. During the two-day wait, SS Captain Wahl—on his own initiative—gathered tanks from all sources (remnants of 2d SS, 9th SS, and 2d Panzer Divisions) and later joined with the 1st SS Panzer Division, which later became known as *Kampfgruppe* Mohnke.[30] This unit caused XV Corps five hard days fighting to reach its objective, which was 20 miles up the Seine.

As in the first envelopment attempt at Falaise, the XIX TAC once again played a role in the reduction of forces attempting to escape the noose at the Seine. Like Patton, XIX TAC was not in awe of the retreating Germans: "West of Paris, too, the Germans were retreating, many crossing the virtually bridge-less Seine during the night by pontoon, by ferry, and even by swimming. At the ferry slips our planes dropped delay-fused bombs set for detonation during the night, at the probable peak of the hurried, nocturnal exodus of supermen."[31] At Third Army the veil of the fearsome Germans was gone. XIX TAC attempted to increase the costs of the German retreat. It destroyed units that were denied XV Corps due to army boundary problems. Eventually, the delayed ground forces were involved in an unnecessary battle with well-prepared and dug-in German forces. Although the envelopment on the Seine failed to secure the lofty goals it once promised, airpower's achievements left a great impression on the enemy, as one German general recalled, "Field Marshal Model had ordered the withdrawal of Fifth Panzer Army across the lower Seine . . . With a tremendous effort, and with the sacrifice of vast quantities of equipment as a result of ceaseless air attacks, the crossing too was completed much against expectations. The last armored formation across was 116th Panzer Division, in the Rouen area. The scene along the banks of the Seine was appalling. Hundreds of smashed vehicles and burned out tanks marked the route which the last German troops had taken."[32] XV Corps eventually closed the gap, but during this drive these troops were turned over to the temporary control of the First US Army. This changed Patton's focus to the south. This transfer also absolved Patton from the time-consuming responsibilities of liberating Paris, which allowed him to continue his dash towards the makeshift defenses in the Paris–Orleans Gap.

During this drive ULTRA greatly aided the speed and effectiveness of the ground scheme of maneuver by highlighting the weak points along the Seine River. The higher headquarters' delays clearly proved Patton's theories correct about slowing down Allied forces. To make up for these delays, XIX TAC was able to hit the German forces crossing the Seine north of the forward advance of the XV Corps. Although the Germans were able to extricate some of their forces, this crossing was extremely costly. When Model's last rear guard crossed the Seine, it had rescued few more than 100 panzers and assault guns.[33] Higher headquarters interfered with some of Patton's plans; but in the south he would have a much freer hand, which made this operation one of his most successful operations of the war.

Patton's Pursuit in the South

The area below Paris became of significant concern to the Germans because so many of their troops to this point had been caught in either the first or second Allied envelopment. Hitler's infatuation with the sea at Avranches—and his mistaken belief that the *grossen* invasion would come at Calais—

caused him to concentrate his forces in the north. Hitler also believed that the Allies would immediately attempt to liberate Paris. When this did not occur, it made maneuvering units to stop Patton's southern drive even more challenging. ULTRA captured the Germans' concerns as they attempted to remedy the situation in the following 17 August movement order: "OKW orders, all troops and authorities of all branches of the Armed Forces in the area of Army Gruppe G, West of the line Orleans–Clermont Ferrand–Montpellier—are, in so far as not projected for defense of fortresses and fortress areas and except for fighting troops of 19th Army, to transfer beginning at once behind the line Seine–Yonne–Bourgogne."[34] On 20 August XII Corps was tasked to beat these German reinforcements, with the initial objective being the Yonne River at Sens. These attacks were predicated on speed, but XII Corps's new commander spent the majority of this operation nervously questioning his commander's tactics.

Patton was very depressed about having to relieve XII Corps commander, Maj Gen Gilbert Cook, but he had blood circulation problems that made even walking difficult. Cook's replacement was Maj Gen Manton Eddy. Eddy was the former commander of the 9th Division and a veteran of the hedgerow fighting. He was not accustomed to Patton's style of warfare, as Patton disclosed in a letter to his wife: "Manton Eddy who took over Doc's [Cook's] corps asked me when I told him his job: 'How much shall I have to worry about my flank?' I told him that depended on how nervous he was. He has been thinking [that] a mile a day [was] good going. I told him to go fifty and he turned pale."[35]

Eddy's concern for his flanks was not ill founded. His corps was on the southernmost flank of Patton's army, and this position was also the southern flank of the Allied front in northern France. Therefore, Eddy was essentially responsible for the flank guard for the Allied effort in Western Europe. This fact caused numerous discussions on the subject that many members of the Third Army staff recalled vividly. Colonel Koch remembered one phone call in which Eddy complained that Patton's plans left his flanks insecure. Patton did not agree and reminded him "in the academic days at Fort Leavenworth, the approved measure was to protect the army's flank by a squadron of horse cavalry, less Troop A. And you've got a da--ed sight more than that."[36] Unfortunately, Eddy did not understand the force-enhancing measures that Patton was using to secure his flanks.

General Harkins (Patton's deputy chief of staff) provided insight into Patton's force-enhancing measures when he related the following story.

> Then we were going across France, General Eddy who had the XII Corps [which] only had four divisions. He was stretched out 80 miles. He had just come from 9th Division up in the hedgerows, and he was really frightened to death because his flanks were wide open. He called General Patton, and said, "Listen, your G-2 tells me there are 90,000 Germans on my right and 80,000 on my left and I've only got four divisions." And General Patton says, "Ignore the ba--ards, go ahead." Then he called O. P. Weyland and told him to watch the flanks, and if anything was coming up the roads to let him know, and then we'd see what we could do.[37]

Patton also confirmed Harkins's words and his reliance on airpower in the book *War As I Knew It*. In relating a similar conversation, Patton provided much of the rationale behind his decisions.

> When this move started, Eddy of the XII Corps asked me how much he should worry about his right flank. I said that depended on how nervous he was by nature. Of course, there was nothing to cover his right flank, but by advancing in depth—that is, one division following the other—this lack of defense was immaterial. If I had worried about flanks, I could have never fought the war. Also, I was convinced that our Air Service could locate any groups of enemy large enough to be a serious threat, and then I could always pull something out of the hat to drive them back while the Air Force in the meantime delayed their further advance.[38]

The forces that Eddy was most concerned with were the German troops who were receiving transfer orders to fill the Paris–Orleans gap. These movement directives were well monitored by ULTRA, as one Bletchley Park employee recalls. "Our output was so great that the movements of most of the major German army and air force units at this time can still be reconstructed with considerable detail from the immense numbers of location reports received, up to a hundred in a single day . . . it [the messages] enabled large staffs which were now working on ULTRA at home and abroad to weave an even tighter intelligence net round the Wehrmacht than before."[39] In 1984 Helfers confirmed Patton's reliance on the vast number of ULTRA messages. Helfers recalled, "He [Patton] got enough information from ULTRA to know there was no danger to his southern flank across the Loire River, it was unheard of that an army would drive through enemy territory without flank guard."[40] Airpower and ULTRA in this scenario turned potential flank guard troops into Patton's spearheads that would lead some of Patton's most successful drives.

Patton's faith in ULTRA and airpower was immense because as Eddy often pointed out, he was gambling the entire flank of the Allied effort in France with this concept. Unfortunately for Eddy, he was not privy to ULTRA information. Patton knew his risks were lowered with the help of ULTRA intelligence. Due to the dutiful German reporting system, Patton knew where the enemy was, where he would be, and in what numbers. These facts were confirmed by conventional sources of intelligence that allowed Patton to apply the correct force allotments to the German weak and strong points. Any unforeseen German countermoves could be rapidly dealt with by airpower that would provide Patton additional time to reorient forces. The air-ground team then could deal efficiently with whatever flank threat that materialized.

Although Eddy had some apprehensions, his XII Corps prosecuted Patton's plan to the letter, which caused Patton to call this operation "the fastest and biggest pursuit in history."[41] XII Corps drove to Montargis, found some opposition, immediately bypassed it, crossed the Loing River at Souppes, and rapidly raced to Sens. This thrust was so quick and unexpected—and the spearheads of XII Corps took the German garrison by such surprise—that some officers were strolling the streets in dress uniform. These unfortunate sightseers missed the last truck home that day, and they witnessed Third Army's capture of their bridgehead on the Yonne.[42] Eddy then telephoned to proclaim: "General, I had a lovely drive. I'm in Sens. What's next?" Patton replied: "Hang up and keep going."[43]

As the infantry routed the bypassed forces in Montargis, Eddy did "keep going"; and his 4th Armored Division drove 40 miles to the outskirts of Troyes, defeating the German forces there in a day. By the time the Allies celebrated the liberation of Paris (25 August), Patton already had four bridgeheads across the Seine; and his forces were almost 80 miles beyond the French capital (map 6). This rapid drive was significantly abetted by the synergistic employment of Patton's force enhancers, which were used in both traditional and unconventional roles.

When the Luftwaffe attempted to deny Patton's army the bridgeheads on the Seine, XIX TAC countered these actions with various air superiority missions. While covering XX Corps, XIX TAC broke up an attack by "seventy plus Fw-190s, many carrying bombs" that were "dispersed" before they could hit their targets.[44] On 25 August the Allies launched an attack specifically focused on the German air force in France. This was a joint operation among the various TACs and numbered air forces that used ULTRA to find and destroy enemy aircraft: "The melding of Y intercept [lower grade communications intercepts] with German Air Force operational order and intentions produced excellent results particularly in the Normandy campaign and after the breakthrough where by virtue of 'source' information. The Ninth Air Force was able to carefully follow the retreating Luftwaffe and deal a successful series of blows at the overcrowded German airfields of Eastern France."[45] XIX TAC's target, Beauvais Airfield, was particularly active and highlighted itself in ULTRA traffic with messages such as the following from Field Luftgau stating, "Urgently need M/T [motor transport] fuel in area of Laon and Beauvais. Allotment urgently requested for stepped up operations, increased transfers and urgent transport of ammunition and aircraft fuel . . . [could] jeopardize further operations."[46] XIX TAC destroyed 13 aircraft on the ground at Beauvais. They also engaged 45 more Focke–Wulf (Fw) 190s in the air which increased their kills by an additional 13 and also damaged three others. Overall, Ninth and Eighth Air Force fighters destroyed or damaged 254 planes, with XIX TAC's portion being 67 aircraft in one day. This day led many after-action report writers to call it "the day that broke the back of the German fighter force in France."[47]

The Allied Air Forces were becoming so dominant that both sides were recognizing the large impact they were having on the battlefield. The demoralizing effects it was having on the German troops forced the military governor of France to circulate the

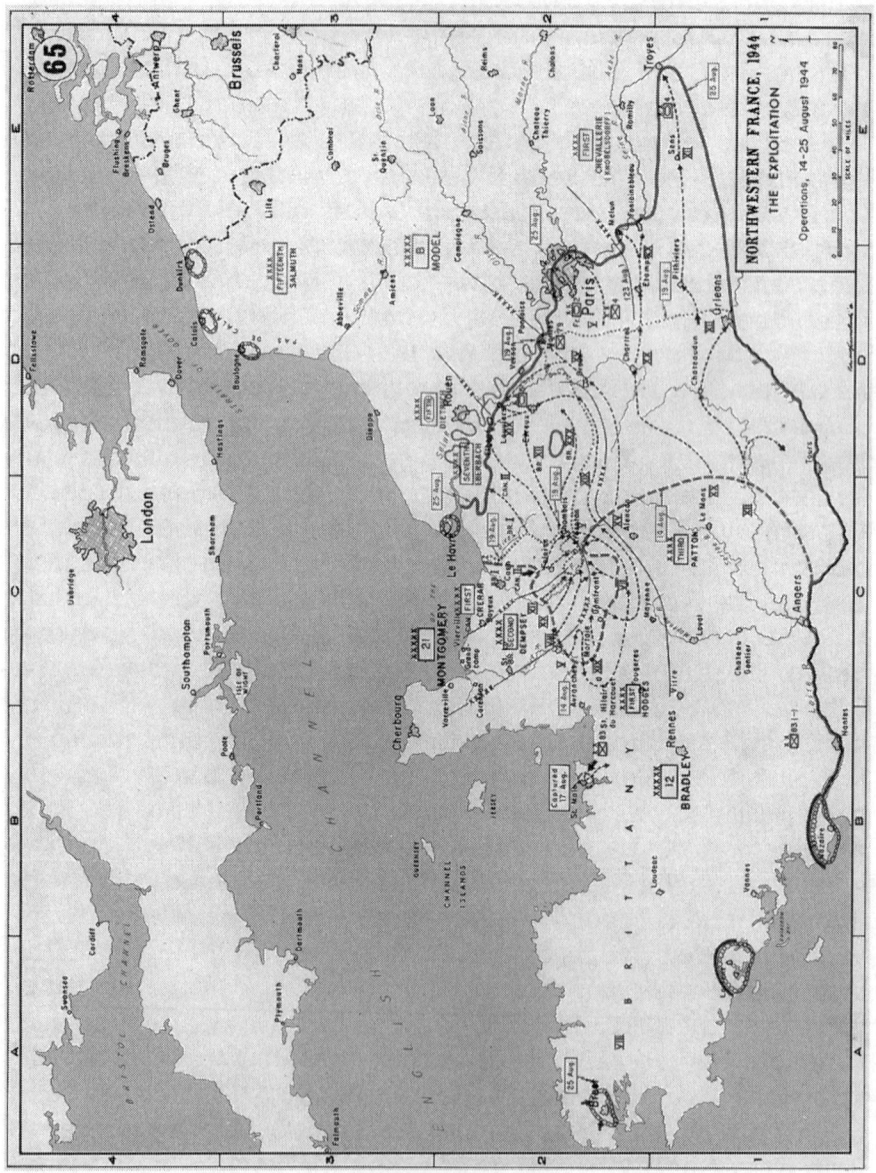

Map 6. Four Seine Bridgeheads and Beyond

following piece of propaganda that was captured during this campaign: "The ground soldier in action on the invasion front feels depressed most of all by enemy air superiority. In spite of the numerical inferiority of our air force, there have been successes accomplished, however, which the single soldier, tied down to his narrow section of the front, cannot appreciate. The following air force information should be known to the troops so that they may know what great support the fighting forces are receiving from their own air force."[48] Unfortunately for the Germans, Patton found one more way for Allied airpower to "depress" the German ground soldiers. In order to keep his eastward drive south of Paris going, Patton became IX Troop Carrier Command's major effort. These C-47s were being held in reserve for possible airborne operations at Chartres and Orleans. Patton's capture of these cities freed them to support other Third Army activities. Patton's LOCs were stretched, and his tanks needed gas and oil. The Red Ball Express (the theater truck-borne delivery system) was having trouble keeping up with Third Army's advances; therefore, Patton again turned to airpower to solve some of his ground-based problems. IX Troop Carrier Command alleviated some of the supply problems associated with Third Army's rapid drives. This support peaked on 26 August with the IX Troop Carriers employing 606 C-47s and three C-53s that transported 2.15 million pounds of fuel and rations.[49] Patton had found another way for airpower to support his ground scheme of maneuver, but the air arm's crowning accomplishment would soon be realized south of the Loire River.

The drive to the Seine was a classic example of Patton using every available asset to exploit the disorganization that was prevalent throughout the retreating German forces. During this American blitzkrieg, Patton employed the tactic of bypassing strong points and attacking weak points deep in the enemy's rear areas. The XIX TAC ULTRA team identified threats and essentially provided a map for the ground scheme of maneuver to guide the ground troops efficiently to the undefended rear. Weyland's airmen provided flank support and cover for the Third Army's spearheads and struck the retreating Germans attempting to cross the Seine. Before Patton's forces initiated their drive to the Seine, Patton wrote his wife:

"Unless I get a stop order in the next two hours, we are jump-ing again. On paper it looks very risky but I don't think it is."[50] The force-enhancing capabilities of ULTRA and the excellent working relationship with XIX TAC do not appear on paper, while history shows that this drive was not risky; and clearly Patton's strategy was sound because in this campaign "no army had ever moved with such speed and dash."[51]

Support Roles Switch—XIX TAC Bags 20,000 Germans

After the fall of Paris on 25 August 1944, Third Army ad-vanced along a 90-mile front that ran along the Loire River—giving Patton a combined flank and front of 450 miles.[52] Patton did not have sufficient forces to cover this vast area ad-equately, thus he became increasingly dependent on XIX TAC and ULTRA. During the early planning in England, Patton told Koch that he had no intention of pushing south of the Loire. This position did not change during the August operations. On 3 August, 12th Army Group specifically directed the Third Army to drive as far south as "the Loire River and protect the right flank with minimum forces as necessary."[53]

This situation initially appeared amenable to both sides. ULTRA and the XIX TAC monitored the German forces south of Loire who reported the "successful demolition of [the] Maine and Loire Bridge near Angers" or "Loire Bridge at LaRoche–Bernard demolished."[54] Considering these were flank-protecting actions, the Germans were merely reducing the target list for the XIX TAC. These German forces were in-corporating some of the same economy-of-force measures that Third Army was employing, as one unit south of the Loire re-ported, "North bank of Loire from Saumar to Nantes being given up to economize forces."[55] For the first two and one-half weeks of August, the forces south of the Loire were clearly fo-cused on defense and holding ground. Patton knew this and could confidently disregard them. The continuous German ref-erences to defensive taskings to "block Loire crossing[s] as far as Tours" showed that they had their attention focused else-where.[56] On 15 August the situation in southern France changed, and these defensive forces rapidly attempted to fill empty gaps in their northern lines in order to avoid another envelopment.

Seventh US Army's invasion of southern France quickly put the German troops south of Loire in a vise. Third Army's rapid drive east along the banks of the Loire, complemented with Seventh Army's drive north up the Rhone valley, put the Germans in the position of being cut off. This led Hitler to send the following message to the commander-in-chief west: "As the development of the situation with Army Group Baker makes the cutting off of [the] 19th Army within a foreseeable period seem possible, [I] order that firstly, Army Group G, with the exception of the forces remaining in Toulon and Marseilles, will disengage from the Allies and will gain contact with the south wing of Army Group B. Construction of an intermediate line Sens–Dijon–Swiss Frontier to be initiated immediately."[57] Additional ULTRA messages provided the routes of these re-treating forces. The order that "railways [were] to be fully used" further aided XIX TAC's interdiction campaign.[58] These railways would become the targets in an operation against the forces south of the Loire.

The following public affairs release of December 1944 clearly displayed Patton's reliance on the XIX TAC. "Never in military history had a ground commander entrusted the defense of an army flank to tactical aircraft, but when Third Army turned east and headed for Paris they left only light holding forces along the Loire River. South of the Loire, General Erich Elster had an estimated 36,000 German troops who could have stabbed viciously into the exposed Third Army flank."[59] Although these forces could have attacked the Third Army flank, the ULTRA audience knew that they had an alternate destination. Numerous intercepted messages directed these forces to the Swiss frontier, and some specifically called the units "to be brought back to [the] area [of] Belfort."[60] With this knowledge, Patton's attitude towards flank guards does not seem particularly brash. At the beginning of this campaign, Patton told Weyland, "I am going to forget completely about my flank if you can guarantee to protect me from the air"; and Weyland agreed saying "I can do that if I have the weather."[61]

As added insurance, Patton knew ULTRA could see through any weather; and the battle south of the Loire became a XIX TAC and ULTRA affair.

Weyland's planners wasted no time. On 23 August they submitted plans to destroy any hopes for the 36,000 Germans to reenter the fight (map 7). Unlike the public affairs release, the XIX TAC planners had a better idea of the desired route for the German forces. The plan was a classic interdiction effort with several phases, which are described in the following passage.

> The success of the American Seventh Army's landing on the Mediterranean coast of France will, or already has, forced a general abandonment by the enemy of his position in Southern France. He must withdraw or be cut off. In withdrawal he has two alternatives. One is to bring his forces north and attack the Third Army's right flank, and the other is to race the Third Army to the German–Swiss corner near Belfort, and if he wins [they will] help set up a defensive line for the protection of the Reich with these forces. It is thought that the latter is the more probable course but whatever the choice, he must use railroads and roads to the utmost. The plan presented herein seeks to deny to him the use of the former and force him to the roads where he will be required to use his badly diminished stocks of oil. The roads and the columns on them in turn should be attacked at points to be chosen as his movements are found.[62]

Due to the meticulous German reporting system, XIX TAC had no trouble finding acceptable targets. Grove specifically highlighted ULTRA's contribution to this campaign by stating, "When Patton's open flank was along the Loire River and XIX TAC was assigned the job of protecting that extended open flank, ULTRA's knowledge of enemy locations and movement was of great value."[63]

The following day the XIX TAC initiated the plan. The 371st Fighter Group reported that it did "a little working on the railroad" along Loire.[64] The initial phase of the scheme made a series of 18 rail cuts and 16 bridge cuts that isolated the forces from the Third Army right flank and severed the northwest route to the German–Swiss border (see map 7).[65] Early in the movement, the German forces employed march tactics and reporting procedures that greatly aided the targeting process as the following message shows, "Danger from [the] Allies and [the] composition of march groups, consider [it] necessary to march main body as one formation. Employment of blocking formations on a line La Charite–Bourges and towards north intended

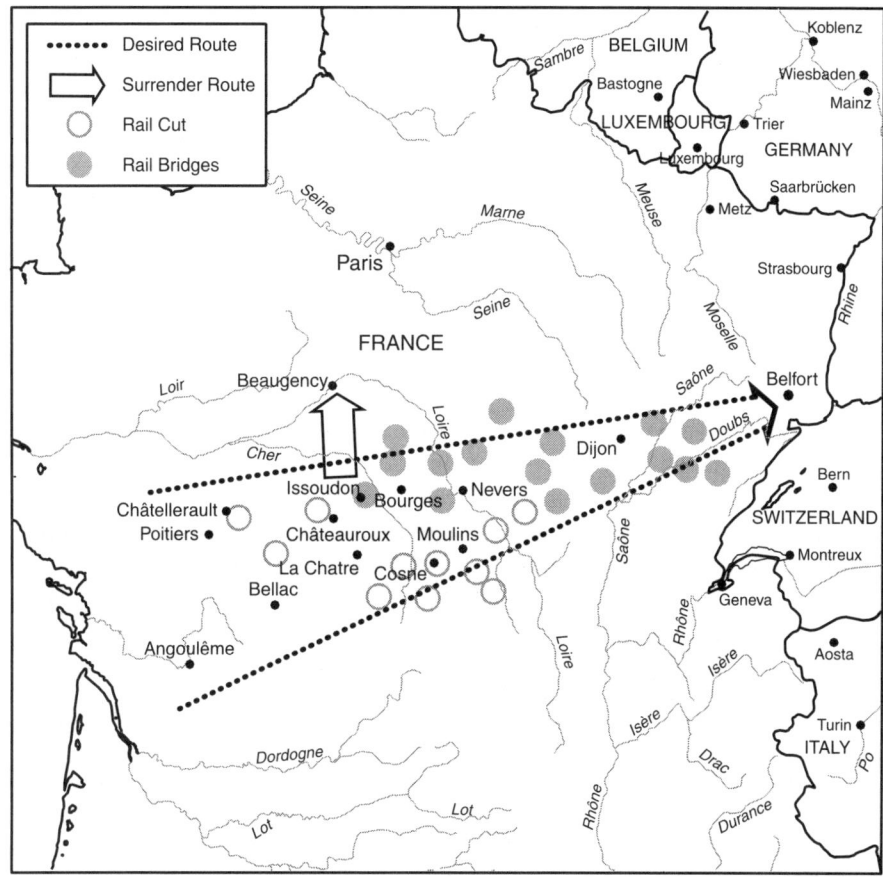

Map 7. XIX Tactical Air Command's Interdiction Plans for the Loire

[the German–Swiss Border] . . . completion of movement by 15 September presuming all runs smoothly."[66] Unfortunately for the Germans, all did not go smoothly. ULTRA indicated the effects of the XIX TAC's denial of rail transport in the following message: "railways cannot be used to [an] advantage because of increasing demolitions. Great strain on persons unaccustomed to marching, in present oppressive heat."[67] With rail movements significantly degraded, the XIX TAC was then ready to transition to targeting individual German units.

Although the area below the Loire River is vast, ULTRA significantly narrowed the search patterns. ULTRA messages tracked the proposed withdrawal routes, which in turn provided the P-47's flight paths for armed reconnaissance missions. One example of the detail provided in these messages comes from the 64th Corps in a message from 26 August: "Routes 'ABLE' Poitiers, La Châtre, Moulins. 'BAKER' Châtellerault, Châteauroux, Bourges, Loire crossing at Nevers, La Chârite, and Cosne. Assembling area [at Châteauroux–Angoulême–Poitiers with last elements of southern group in Angoulême on 1 September. Loire crossing with first elements [of] main body probably not before 12 September."[68] The movement of the German troops started to demand action on the last days of August. The following message provided the area of operations for XIX TAC's armed reconnaissance missions: "Covering forces on [the] Loire until last elements of 159 Reserve Division pass[es] through Angoulême–Poitiers area. South of Châteauroux–Poitiers line, thrust to east reveal strong guerrilla crossings and destruction of bridges, which with difficult terrain are delaying progress. Thus Poitiers turning point for all elements streaming back."[69]

On 1 September XIX TAC specifically targeted the above area of interest, and the air strikes scored immediate results as the XIX TAC's daily intelligence summary reports: "36th Group flew 4 armed recce missions south of the Loire River in the Poitiers–Châteauroux–Bourges area. One of these, a group mission, with 35 aircraft participating, provided the highlight of the day with the destruction of 311 MT [motor transports] and 94 armored vehicles. The 53d Squadron of this Group attacked an ammunition dump near Poitiers and reported explosions from it that continued for 15 minutes after the attack."[70] XIX TAC continued these attacks below the Loire for the next 10 days. The targets often corresponded to the specific locations cited in the ULTRA messages. The Germans continued to report their progress, and the XIX TAC made sure they would not make their proposed schedule. The 64th Corps, who were heading for the Swiss border, stated that they "intended to cross the Loire on the ninth [September]"; and their Army Group instructed them "to expedite this if possible."[71] Following this message, XIX TAC had one of its best days, reporting on 7 September:

406th Group, in two armed recces in the Chateauroux–Issoudun–
Bourges area provided the high spot of the day. Upon receipt of a
Tac/R report that an enemy column was moving in that area, 406th
Group was sent out on the target, found the column, and bombed and
strafed it until their ammunition was exhausted. Returning to base for
more ammunition they hurried back to the target and completed the
destruction of the entire column. Pilots reported that French civilians
were taking the few remaining vehicles in the column as our aircraft
left. Total claims: 132 motor transport and 310 horse-drawn vehicles
destroyed or damaged.[72]

After three additional days of air attacks, the Germans south
of the Loire were ready to quit. German General Elster sent a
note through messengers to the closest ground units that his
forces were done. General Elster stated his terms for surrender as: "Keep the 'Jabo' (German slang for fighter-bomber—
Jagdbomber) off my men and they will march north to
Beaugency bridge and surrender."[73]

Since these German troops were more than 250 miles behind Patton's forward line of troops, the Ninth US Army (the
closest ground units to the Germans) sent representatives to
discuss the formal terms of surrender. Information from this
meeting rapidly demonstrated the effects of airpower because
the Germans "insisted that Weyland, whose planes had
caused him so much anguish, be at the ceremony."[74] Because
these troops were so far from any ground units, the 20,000
Germans were instructed to change their northeast route and
march under a white flag directly north to the Beaugency
bridge. Weyland then sent the Germans a note saying, "Okay,
we'll keep you under surveillance, and if you make a false
move, you'll get hit again."[75]

Gen William H. Simpson, Ninth US Army commander, was
confused by the German ground troops' request involving
Weyland; therefore, he drove to XIX TAC headquarters to get
some answers. Although the only US forces that engaged the
Germans were the XIX TAC, General Simpson was still per-
plexed by a note given to him by one of his subordinate generals. Weyland fondly remembered Simpson's education in the
abilities of airpower in the following story:

So Baldy Simpson said that he got that message from a German general through his division commander, who said that they wanted to
turn in their suits if they would quit hitting them from the air. Well, it

just happened the day before, or the morning of that same day. He was down there one afternoon and said, "What's the meaning of all this?" I said, "Well, I just got some wet prints of these German troops south about 100 miles, or something like that. They're getting a little desperate, and they're trying to move. They've formed up in columns and [are] trying to head back toward Germany. It just so happened we caught about two columns, each about ten miles long . . . We just got through beating the he-- out of them this morning, and here happens to be the pictures." Well, on these roads there were burning trucks and vehicles and whatnot. Smoke [was] moving up. Some vehicles were trying to get off the roads into the fields to get away. And he looked at that, and said, "My God, now I understand. That's why the old boy wants to quit. I don't blame him."[76]

After this educational session, General Simpson decided not to attend the formal surrender ceremony. This became a wise decision because the major general that Simpson sent took a backseat to Weyland.

The 83d Infantry Division was responsible for all facets of the ceremony. The 83d ensured that the formal protocol for the ceremony would dictate that General Elster would surrender to Maj Gen Robert C. Macon (the 83d Division commander). To guarantee there was no confusion, the 83d protocol representatives provided the following scripts in German and English to make sure all items ran smoothly:

General Elster: "Forced by the war situation, it was decided by the High Command to withdraw the combat troops from my March Group. Therefore I am unable to make a breakthrough to the German Frontier by force of arms, I herewith surrender the ground and supply troops remaining with me to the Ninth US Army, in accordance with mutually agreed terms." General hands over a weapon as a symbol. Major General [Macon]: "On behalf of the Army of United States, I accept your surrender. You and your command will receive fair treatment as prisoners of war."[77]

Unfortunately, the Germans did not agree with the script and did not let their concerns be known until during the ceremony. Breaking ranks with protocol, General Elster disregarded General Macon and walked over to the XIX TAC commander and in Weyland's words: "He turned over his pistol to me, not the Army General."[78] The assistant Third Army G-2 shares a similar story related to the snub of the Ninth US Army. Although Third Army's ground troops never engaged the German forces south of the Loire, the air-ground teamwork under Patton was highlighted by General Elster's unrehearsed

Surrender Ceremonies at Beaugency Bridge

speech, which is reflected in Col Robert Allen's recollections of the event:

> Two hundred and fifty miles in the rear of Lucky's [Third Army's] line of contact, 64th German Corps had decided to call it quits. Several days before the formal capitulation, this portion of Third Army's far-flung zone was suddenly transferred to Ninth Army. Without having raised a finger to force surrender, Ninth Army collected some 20,000 Krauts and their Lugers. To Third Army men the loss of the latter was even more painful than the juicy PW bag. But there was one hilarious compensation. The surrender formalities took place in an ancient little town of Beaugency, on the Loire 30 miles southwest of Orleans . . . Major General Robert C. Macon, CG 83d Infantry Division, Brigadier General O. P. Weyland, CG XIX TAC, and other senior officers were present. As part of the ceremony, Elster made a speech. When he concluded, an interpreter was asked what the Kraut said. The interpreter fidgeted, hemmed and hawed. "Well, what did he say?" was demanded. "Couldn't you understand him?" "Yes, sir," replied the interpreter. "I understood him all right. He said he wanted it clearly understood that he was surrendering to the Third US Army."[79]

The surrender at Beaugency represented an example of the ground scheme of maneuver supporting an interdiction campaign that delayed, disrupted, and then destroyed forces that capitulated under the threat of further air strikes. In turn, the force-enhancing effects of airpower and ULTRA provided Patton assurances that his flank was not at risk, which provided more troops that could be used as spearheads.

Some historians see the Seine and Loire campaigns through the nervous eyes of General Eddy. They highlight Patton's hard-driving campaign, but they also fault him for his apparent risky maneuvers. Patton's biographer, Martin Blumenson, characterized this campaign as "reckless exploitation"; but with the declassification of ULTRA and the knowledge of Patton's reliance on airpower, his actions seem much less brazen.[80] Patton's AOR was growing exponentially, and he had to find force enhancers to ensure his drive eastward could continue. Patton knew any delays in his drive towards the Rhine would allow his enemies time to prepare defenses and would close the window of opportunity that existed during this period. The combination of operational necessity; detailed, timely, and very accurate knowledge of enemy capabilities and intentions; and a cooperative air element whose commander was fully attuned to Patton's maneuver philosophy and style of war produced a situation that allowed Patton to exploit fully the potential synergies of air-ground operations.

These synergies enabled Patton's forces to drive within 60 miles of the German border. But in the next phase of operations, the Allies were finally able to accomplish something the Germans were never able to do—they stopped the air-ground team of the Third Army.

Notes

1. Oscar W. Koch and Robert G. Hays, *G-2: Intelligence for Patton* (Philadelphia: Whitmore Publishing, 1971), 53.

2. Ibid., 53–54.

3. Martin Blumenson, *The Patton Papers,* vol. 2, *1940–1945* (Boston: Houghton Mifflin, 1974), 503.

4. Great Britain Public Record Office, "ULTRA: Main Series of Signals Conveying Intelligence," Bletchley Park, 1944, reel 35, XL 5533. Copy located in Auburn University Library, Auburn, Ala.

5. Ibid., XL 5619.

6. O. P. Weyland, Report 168.7104-1—"Weyland Diary—XIX TAC" (Albert F. Simpson Historical Research Center: Weyland Collection, 18 May 1945), diary for 13 August 1944, entry 0900.

7. Great Britain Public Record Office, reel 36, XL 6121.

8. Ibid., XL 6188.

9. Blumenson, 510.

10. George S. Patton Jr., "General Patton's Own Story," *Saturday Evening Post,* 1 November 1947, 16.

11. Martin Blumenson, *Breakout and Pursuit* (Washington, D.C.: Office of the Chief of Military History, Department of the Army, 1961), 566.

12. XIX TAC Staff, Report 168.7104-64—"Twelve Thousand Fighter-Bomber Sorties" (Albert F. Simpson Historical Research Center: Weyland Collection, 30 September 1944), 20.

13. Blumenson, *Breakout and Pursuit*, 571.

14. XIX TAC Staff, "Twelve Thousand Fighter-Bomber Sorties," 23.

15. Ralph Francis Bennett, *ULTRA in the West: The Normandy Campaign, 1944–45* (New York: Scribner Co., 1980), 119.

16. Melvin C. Helfers, video tape interview at The Citadel (Charleston, S.C.: The Citadel Archives, 9 October 1984).

17. Blumenson, *Breakout and Pursuit*, 563.

18. Ibid., 569.

19. Ibid., 573–74.

20. Great Britain Public Record Office, reel 36, XL 6648.

21. Ibid., XL 6495.

22. Great Britain Public Record Office, reel 35, XL 5834.

23. Third US Army, "After Action Report, 1 Aug 44–9 May 45," vol. 1, Annex N, Third US Army Directives, Regensburg, Germany, 1945, VII. Copy located in Auburn University Library, Auburn, Ala.

24. Great Britain Public Record Office, reel 37, XL 6814.

25. Blumenson, *Breakout and Pursuit*, 573.

26. Blumenson, *The Patton Papers*, 521–22.

27. Ibid., 522.

28. Ibid., 542–43.

29. Blumenson, *Breakout and Pursuit*, 578.

30. Ibid.

31. XIX TAC Staff, "Twelve Thousand Fighter-Bomber Sorties," 26.

32. Seymour Freidin, Werner Kreipe, and William Richardson, eds., *The Fatal Decisions* (New York: W. Sloan Associates, 1956) 230–31.

33. Ronald Lewin, *ULTRA Goes to War: The First Account of World War II's Greatest Secret Based on Official Documents* (London: Hutchinson Co., 1978), 345.

34. Great Britain Public Record Office, reel 37, XL 6753.

35. Blumenson, *The Patton Papers*, 522.

36. Koch and Hays, 162.

37. James Hasdorff, Report K239.0512-522—"Interview with General Paul D. Harkins" (Air Force Historical Research Center: Corona Harvest Collection, 23 February 1972), 7.

38. George S. Patton Jr., Paul D. Harkins, and Beatrice A. Patton, *War as I Knew It* (Boston: Houghton Mifflin, 1947), 113.

39. Bennett, 136.

40. Helfers interview, 9 October 1984.

41. Martin Blumenson, *Patton: The Man behind the Legend, 1885–1945* (New York: Morrow, 1985), 233.

42. Blumenson, *Breakout and Pursuit*, 584.

43. Carlo D'Este, *Patton: A Genius for War* (New York: HarperCollins Publishers, 1995), 637.

44. XIX TAC Staff, "Twelve Thousand Fighter-Bomber Sorties," 21.

45. John C. Griggs, SRH-023—"Reports by US Army ULTRA Representatives in the European Theater of Operations" (National Archives: Record Group 457, 17 May 1945), 2.

46. Great Britain Public Record Office, reel 37, XL 7348.

47. XIX TAC Staff, "Twelve Thousand Fighter-Bomber Sorties," 29.

48. Ibid., 22.

49. IX Troop Carrier Command Staff, Report K110.7006-2—"Special Project File" (Albert F. Simpson Historical Research Center: Research Studies Institute, 30 November 1944), 2.

50. Blumenson, *The Patton Papers*, 522.

51. Blumenson, *Patton: The Man behind the Legend*, 233.

52. Koch and Hays, 66.

53. Third US Army, "After Action Report, 1 Aug 44–9 May 45," vol. 1, Annex 1, Twelfth US Army Group Directives, Regensburg, Germany, 1945, 2. Copy located in Auburn University Library, Auburn, Ala.

54. Great Britain Public Record Office, reels 35 and 36, XL 5794 and XL 6636.

55. Ibid., reel 36, XL 5704.

56. Ibid., XL 6188.

57. Ibid., XL 6919.

58. Ibid., reel 37, XL 7171.

59. O. P. Weyland, Report 168.7104-101—"Fly, Seek and Destroy" (Albert F. Simpson Historical Research Center: Weyland Collection, 13 December 1944), 3.

60. Great Britain Public Record Office, reel 37, XL 7246, XL 7296, and XL 7471.

61. Office of the Assistant Chief of Air Staff for Intelligence, Report 168.7104-92—"IMPACT—US Tactical Air Power in Europe" (Albert F. Simpson Historical Research Center: Weyland Collection, May 1945), 28.

62. XIX TAC Staff, Report 168.7104-85—"Operation Plan: Air Support of Third Army's Drive to the East" (Albert F. Simpson Historical Research Center: Weyland Collection, 23 August 1944), 1.

63. Harry M. Grove, SRH-023—"Reports by US Army ULTRA Representatives in the European Theater of Operations" (National Archives: Record Group 457, 30 May 1945), 5.

64. XIX TAC Staff, "Twelve Thousand Fighter-Bomber Sorties," 28.

65. XIX TAC Staff, "Operation Plan: Air Support of Third Army's Drive to the East," 1–2.

66. Great Britain Public Record Office, reel 38, XL 7518.

67. Ibid., XL 8240.

68. Ibid., XL 7955.

69. Ibid., reel 39, XL 8390.

70. XIX TAC Staff, Report 168.7104-82—"XIX Tactical Air Command Daily Intelligence Summary" (Albert F. Simpson Historical Research Center: Weyland Collection, 2 September 1944), 2.

71. Great Britain Public Record Office, reel 40, XL 9089.

72. XIX TAC Staff, "XIX Tactical Air Command Daily Intelligence Summary," 8 September 1944, 2.

73. XIX TAC Staff, Report 168.7104-90—"XIX TAC—Tactical Air Operations in Europe" (Albert F. Simpson Historical Research Center: Weyland Collection, May 1945), 48.

74. Office of the Assistant Chief of Air Staff for Intelligence, Report 168.7104-92, 30.

75. Ralph Stephenson, Report K239.0512-813—"Interview with General O. P. Weyland" (Air Force Historical Research Center: Weyland Collection, 19 November 1974), 78–79.

76. Ibid., 80.

77. Jules K. French, Report 168.7104-38—"Report of Activities of Liaison Officer with German Marsch Gruppe Sud" (Air Force Historical Research Center: Weyland Collection, 20 September 1944), appendix 1.

78. Stephenson.

79. Robert S. Allen, *Lucky Forward* (New York: Vanguard Press, 1947), 144–45.

80. Blumenson, *The Patton Papers*, 528.

Chapter 6

Allies Back the Wrong Horse—Patton's Cavalry Stopped

We have, at this time, the greatest chance to win the war ever presented. If they will let me move on with three Corps, two up, one back, on the line of Metz–Nancy–Epinal, we can be in Germany in 10 days. There are plenty of roads and railroads to support the operation. It can be done with three armored and six infantry divisions. It is such a sure thing that I fear these blind moles don't see it.

—Gen George S. Patton Jr.

The quick capitulation of Paris on 25 August 1944 denied the Germans the time they needed to build secondary defenses beyond the Seine. One week earlier, the CINC west and the German military governor of France were directing the "most rapid provision of manpower to develop the Somme–Marne–Saône–Jura [defensive] positions"; but all of these positions were rapidly overrun.[1] General Patton's forces south of Paris sent the German forces reeling towards their border, and many felt the Nazis were on the verge of collapse. After the Normandy campaign, the Germans assessed that they had "the equivalent of 27 divisions," with their "tank establishment particularly low," facing 53 full-strength Allied divisions with five additional divisions dedicated to the fortresses in Brittany.[2] Many of the Allies felt that the Germans were kaput and believed that any single push would cause Germany's downfall. This cockiness led to questionable courses of action that confounded Patton. He saw what appeared to be an obvious opportunity to shorten the war turn into an ill-advised airborne operation that destroyed his entrée to the German heartland.

Once the Allies were beyond the Seine, the next main objective became the Rhine River. Allied planners saw that there were four basic routes into Germany. These four routes were analyzed geographically with the choices varying between (1) the easily flooded flatlands of Flanders; (2) another route via Amiens, Maubeuge, and Liège along the northern edge of the Ardennes; (3) a path through the hilly woodland of the Ardennes; or (4) the road south of the Ardennes through Metz, the Saar, and Frankfurt. Choices one and three were discarded on the basis of terrain, which led to competing strategies between Patton's route of advance in the south and Montgomery's in the north. General Montgomery presented a myriad of reasons why his route of advance should be the Allied main effort (shortest route to the industrial Ruhr Valley and Berlin, additional seaports, elimination of V-weapon sites, etc.). But General Patton saw many pitfalls in Montgomery's route, and the available evidence confirmed many of Patton's concerns.[3]

The Allies' successive August envelopments to the north channeled the majority of the retreating Germans into Montgomery's northern sector. This action ensured that any drive within Montgomery's section would face the brunt of the surviving German forces. This area also afforded the enemy excellent terrain that was conducive for defensive warfare. Montgomery's initial plans would have affected Patton's ground scheme of maneuver because Montgomery wanted to shift the Allies' emphasis to the northern sector where Patton thought the terrain would not be propitious for his form of tank warfare, as he noted in his diary: "I cannot understand why Monty keeps asking for all four Armies to be in the Calais area and then move through Belgium, where his tanks are practically useless now because of the numerous canals and will be wholly useless this winter. Unfortunately, he has some way of talking Ike [Gen Dwight D. Eisenhower, supreme allied commander] into his own way of thinking."[4] Montgomery's initial August request to concentrate the Allied forces in his sector was denied by General Eisenhower, who at this time favored a simultaneous broad-front approach. This denial allowed Patton to continue his ground scheme of maneuver to the east.

The last week of August saw the Third Army continue its string of rapid successes. With the Germans consolidated in either Montgomery's northern sector or retreating from southern France, there was a large gap in the German lines opposite the Third Army's positions. The Germans' situation during this time frame was tenuous. As one German general pointed out, the idea of defensive positions was contrary to any of Hitler's initiatives.

> The reader will frequently have wondered why there were no prepared defensive positions into which the army might have been withdrawn . . . The answer is that in Hitler's eyes such foresight was a cardinal sin. Nobody was even allowed so much as to contemplate the possibility of a withdrawal, and the provision of a defensive line to the rear of the battle zone might, he felt, encourage such thoughts . . . It is true that, as a top secret matter, the possibility of forming a line running from the Somme along the line of the Marne and the Saone . . . had been investigated in theory. But no such line had been constructed and now there were no forces available either to build or to man it. In any event, it was too late, for this theoretical defensive line had been overrun by the enemy in the Marne sector.[5]

The Third Army's rapid movements quickly confirmed the above information as they encountered few enemy troops and even fewer defensive positions. Patton's XX Corps turned over their bridgeheads across the Seine to the First US Army and then proceeded to Reims. Farther to the south, XII Corps traveled from Troyes to Vitry-le-François with little difficulty and then crossed the Marne and took Chalons without encountering any trench lines or notable German resistance. The next target was the Meuse River, and once again the countryside was relatively void of Germans. A light company surprised enemy outposts at Commercy and neutralized their artillery positions by shooting the crews before they could remove their breechblock covers. This action allowed this company to seize the Meuse bridge intact. Third Army continued to destroy disorganized opposition, and by 1 September they had bridgeheads along the Meuse River at Commercy, St. Mihiel, and Verdun (map 8).[6]

The next defensive line in Patton's way was the Siegfried Line (known to the Germans as the West Wall). During the previous four years, this defensive line received less attention than the imaginary Somme–Marne–Saône line. The Germans stripped these fortifications for the sake of the Atlantic Wall, and its condition in August 1944 was pathetic. Von

Map 8. Attacks to the West Wall

Rundstedt's conviction was "that at this time the Allies could have broken through the West Wall whenever they wished."[7] This fact discomfited the Germans as they made every effort to fall back and reenergize their defensive capabilities. ULTRA messages reporting redeployments like: "Early second [of September] Commander-in-Chief West reported intentions . . . [to] transfer Panzer base from Metz to Kaiserslautern" only further encouraged Patton's forces toward their intermediate target—the Moselle River.[8]

During this drive Patton experienced the effects of differing priorities from higher headquarters. Montgomery convinced Eisenhower that portions of Third Army's gas supply should go north to support his drive. Therefore, starting on 23 August, Patton's gas rations began to decrease. Patton was able to make up some of these shortfalls through the capture of German fuel, but Montgomery's increased demands stifled even these efforts. Unfortunately, this misallocation of resources eventually eroded the various force-enhancing capabilities that Patton had depended upon in previous campaigns.

As August drew to a close, Montgomery became more successful at swaying Eisenhower. The broad-front initiative started to become unrealistic, and the Allies' solution was to make drastic cuts in Third Army supplies. On 28 August Bradley told Patton the majority of supplies would go to First Army. The latter was now in support of Montgomery's forces, who were heading towards more important objectives; and higher authorities also directed that an additional 3,000 tons of daily supplies would go to the civilians of Paris.[9] This redirection of effort, complemented by Montgomery's upcoming plans, would also eliminate a function of airpower that Third Army had become dependent upon, as Patton complained in the following comment: "In addition to this (the loss of supplies), the airlift, on which we had previously counted for a good proportion of our supplies, was being diverted to feed Parisians; while other transport planes were being assembled . . . for an air drop in front of the Twenty-First Army Group. Finally, as a last straw, Com Z (Communications Zone) used several truck companies to move their headquarters from Cherbourg to Paris at this very date."[10] Patton soon found out that he could expect no additional supplies until 3 September. This information came at the same time the CINC west admitted to *Generaloberst* Alfred Jodl that the Allies had attained absolute tactical superiority and judged them able to avoid lines of defense and capable of "destroying the German military forces in the west."[11] These facts, together with the Third Army's withering logistical support, eventually led Patton to exclaim:

> The twenty-ninth of August was, in my opinion, one of the critical days in this war, and hereafter many pages will be written on it—or, rather, on the events which produced it. It was evident at this time that there was no real threat against us . . . Everything seemed rosy, when suddenly it was reported to me that the 140,000 gallons of gas we were to get that day had not arrived. At first I thought it was a backhanded way of slowing the Third Army. I later found out that this was not the case, but that the delay was due to a change of plan by the High Command, implemented, in my opinion, by General Montgomery . . . I presented my case for a rapid advance to the east for the purpose of cutting the Siegfried Line before it could be manned. Bradley was very sympathetic, but Bull (Major General H. R. Bull, Eisenhower's G-3) and, I gather, the rest of SHAEF's (Supreme Headquarters Allied Expeditionary Force) Staff did not concur. It was my opinion then that this was the momentous error of the war.[12]

Patton's accusations were serious; and after investigating the facts on both sides of the battle lines, it appears that his appraisal may well have been correct.

Patton's frustrations with this situation were similar to every other battle Third Army fought in France. He knew any delay would give the Germans time to fill their gaps and close the window of opportunity. The Germans' attempt to fill the holes in their lines involved the rapid redeployment of their troops from southern France. But Montgomery's meddling was not the only factor that hampered Patton's ability to deal with enemy troops moving up from southern France.

In late August von Rundstedt returned to France and spent much of his time trying to close the hole between the Third Army and the Rhine River. ULTRA intercepted numerous messages encouraging the 19th Army to expedite the movements up the Rhone Valley.[13] These elements were farther to the east from the units that XIX TAC engaged south of Loire. Although the XIX TAC bagged 20,000 prisoners, many more escaped farther to the east because of the numerous delays in supplies and the diversion of the XIX TAC to other areas of interest. Bradley diffused Patton's efforts when he shifted a significant portion of XIX TAC's focus nearly 500 miles to the rear in order to finish the attacks on the port of Brest. Patton recalled this request in the following diary entry: "He [Bradley] said to me, with reference to the Brest operation, 'I would not say this to anyone but you, and have given different excuses to my staff and higher echelons, but we must take Brest in order to maintain the illusion of the fact that the US Army cannot be beaten.' More emotion than I thought he had."[14] Patton fully supported his boss on this emotional issue, but it cost him the force-enhancing capabilities of the XIX TAC at a time when all of Patton's assets were spread extremely thin.

On 2 September Bradley's emphasis on the Brest target also came down through Air Force channels, and General Weyland recorded this fact in a diary entry stating, "call from Gen[eral] Vandenberg—Brest to get highest priority."[15] Unfortunately, this move also could be categorized as another momentous error of the campaign. The biggest fault with this requirement was that it was a tremendous waste of sorties at a critical time. The XIX TAC after-action report clearly demonstrates this sentiment in the following observation:

> The experience of this command has demonstrated clearly that the employment of fighter-bombers against strong fixed fortifications such as Brest is relatively ineffective. Far greater destruction and loss can be inflicted upon the enemy by employing these aircraft against proper fighter-bomber targets such as troops, transport, materiel on the move, supply depots and lines of communications. An example was the series of fighter-bomber attacks on the enemy forces south of the Loire in early September. These attacks culminated in the surrender of a major general and 20,000 troops which had been cut off from escape into Germany . . . The fruits of this program of interdiction and harassment would have been considerably larger had it not been interrupted by the concentration of the fighter-bomber effort at Brest.[16]

The XIX TAC could have been more effectively employed by keeping the gaps in the German lines open by expanding the destruction south of Loire to the units retreating up Rhone Valley. This effort could have aided the sluggish ground scheme of maneuver that was suffering from a lack of supplies. These targets (ground units in travel mode) were the most conducive for fighter-bombers' attacks, and the eradication of these German troops would have made the greatest contribution to the Third Army's efforts. XIX TAC further complained that General Middleton called "for more and more air, . . . in spite of the presence of 31 battalions of artillery."[17] More importantly, the ineffectiveness of fighter-bombers against these targets and the outstanding capabilities of artillery against fixed fortifications were well known before the time Brest was given priority for air assets.

ULTRA provided excellent bomb damage assessment reports through Brest's daily situation reports. Early in the campaign, Brest reported "all phone and teleprinter lines [were] cut," and they had to depend on the wireless Enigma machine to stay in contact with higher headquarters.[18] Numerous ULTRA messages from Brest stated "roofs of pens not pierced" or "no damage or casualties caused by fighter-bomber attack."[19] ULTRA was not the only available intelligence to confirm the shortcomings of fighter-bombers against fortifications. On 21 August the forts at St. Malo fell, and the German POWs "were almost unanimous in stating that it was artillery fire, gradually reducing their defensive guns to a state of helplessness, that brought [their] surrender, and that the air attacks including those in the final phase had no decisive effect."[20] Although all of this evidence was available to Allied senior leadership, it did not stop them from dedicating 400 aircraft, which led to "street fighting with P-47s" where "little progress was made."[21]

Throughout these aerial attacks, German ULTRA messages continued to confirm the object of this operation (the ports of Brest) would be worthless. Situation reports from Brest frequently provided discouraging updates, as in the following report from 4 September: "By late third [of September], demolition completed of all installations at Brest vital to war—railway station, electricity works, etc. and commercial harbor. Demolition of Naval Harbor continuing."[22] The Brest commander reconfirmed on 9 September that the "fortress would be defended by Ramcke (*Generalleutant* Herman B. Ramcke, Brest commander) to the end and [would] only [be] given up to the Allies as a heap of ruins."[23] *Generalleutant* Herman B. Ramcke delivered on his promise and when he surrendered on

19 September, the port of Brest was worthless. Consequently, the Allies decided simply to contain the ports of Lorient, St. Nazaire, and the pocket north of Bordeaux with holding forces

Port of Brest after the German Surrender

until the end of the war. This solution may have been a better course of action regarding Brest during a period when the bulk of XIX TAC was needed elsewhere.

The diversion of airpower had its costs. One reporter specifically asked Patton: "Is the lack of air cover hampering operations now?" Patton confirmed that they were involved in more important operations over Brest.[24] The fact was that the most important operation at that time was the gap 500 miles to the east which was being filled by retreating forces from the Rhone Valley. Bradley's emphasis on Brest further hindered Patton's advances as he attempted to carry on his attack with limited supplies and air cover. XIX TAC knew these retreating forces would be employed in combat again, and with the limited extra resources available they tried to destroy the Germans outside of their AOR, as the following report confirms.

Many troops from this area did manage to escape into Germany before junction was effected between the Third and Seventh US Armies, some of them crossing the Loire in the vicinity of Nevers. Our fighter-bombers covered that area, although it was far south of the Army boundary, in an effort to discourage this withdrawal. Unfortunately, the crucial period in the program of interdiction and harassment coincided with the period of all-out attack on Brest, and because of the priority accorded the latter project, this program was unable to achieve complete success.[25]

The delay of the coupling of Third Army and Seventh Army may have been the most serious breach associated with the diversion of supplies to the north. The only thing that stopped General Patton from sealing off these forces from Germany was a lack of gas and supplies. In late August Patton made this point clear when he wrote to his son: "my chief difficulty is not the Germans but gasoline. If they would give me enough gas, I could go anywhere I want." By mid-September the Third Army and Seventh Army finally met, crushing the German 16th Division between them.[26] But as the XIX TAC had already pointed out, this was only after numerous Germans had escaped the potential losses associated with the bombing exploits of XIX TAC or the envelopment caused by the ground scheme of maneuver of the Third Army.

The choices made during this time frame cost the Allies many opportunities, and no one was more upset than Patton. But these setbacks would pale in comparison to Montgomery's next scheme, which was supported by the Supreme Headquarters Allied Expeditionary Force (SHAEF) staff. Unfortunately, ULTRA would signal a clear pathway into the Third Reich; but Montgomery's newfound audacity would lead him to disregard all warnings that clearly showed the hazards associated with his ill-planned drive in the north. Once again, decisions made beyond Patton's control would force him to make adjustments in his plans to continue his drive toward Germany.

Allies Choose the Road Worst Traveled

Encouraged by Patton's southern drives and Montgomery's rapid gains through Brussels and Antwerp, the Allies began to believe that the Germans were so feeble that they would be incapable of stopping a major Allied thrust. Given this premise, Montgomery offered his leadership and forces to become that major Allied thrust. On 4 September he proposed a plan that called for his forces to receive all of the available resources for a single strong drive to Berlin via the Ruhr. This plan was predicated on stopping the Third Army to support his drive. Eisenhower declined this plan, once again favoring a broad-front strategy; and he also believed that this proposal's strong thrust was pencil-like. Eisenhower then offered ways to strengthen the attack; and Montgomery was granted the use of SHAEF's strategic reserve, the Allied Airborne Army.[27]

On 10 September the Allies backed Montgomery's next plan, which ensured that Patton would not see airlift support for quite awhile. This plan rested on the assumption that Allied airborne troops would seize a series of bridges, while armor forces would advance across 64 miles of enemy territory on a one-tank front—along elevated, unprotected highways—flanked by a soft and sodden tank-proof landscape.[28] Unfortunately, the only Allied personnel who crossed into the Ruhr via this attack were POWs. The accepted theory for the failure of this operation portrays Montgomery as the victim of a huge intelligence catastrophe. An example of this view is Albert A. Nofi's book, *The War against Hitler,* which faulted intelligence in the following manner.

> The Fifteenth (Army) made a bold attempt to evacuate across the Scheldt and the British made no serious effort to cut off their withdrawal. Once they got out, they withdrew north and west of Eindhoven to rest and refit. In addition at about the same time, the German II SS Panzer Corps was pulled out of the Eifel and sent to Arnhem to refit. This put the 9th and 10th SS Panzer Divisions in Arnhem. Both operations, conducted in the early days of September, were carried out rather openly. Yet neither was accounted for in the intelligence summaries upon which the planned operation was based (map 9).[29]

This theory on the failure of intelligence has huge ramifications for the analysis of Patton's actions during this period. If Allied intelligence could not track Panzer corps and divisions, these German units that were unaccounted for could have been opposite Third Army's positions—which would really call into question the genius of Patton's force-enhancing maneuvering with ULTRA. Unfortunately for Montgomery and Nofi,

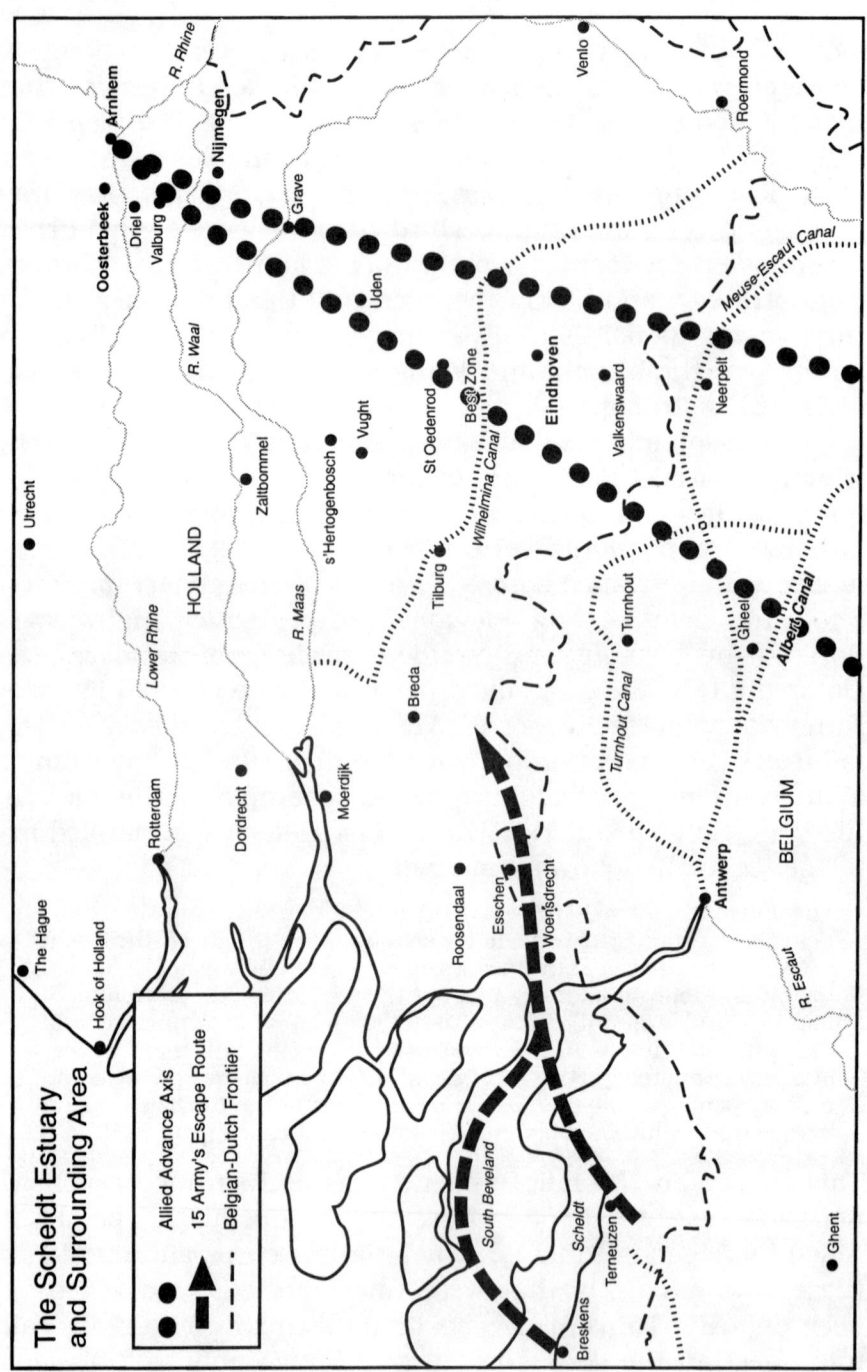

Map 9. Operation Market Garden

the declassification of ULTRA destroys this theory and—more importantly—suggests that the best route into the German heartland was opposite Third Army's positions. In order to support Montgomery's offensive, once again Patton's forces were stalled and his supplies were diverted north. Considering the ULTRA information and the numerous disruptions in Third Army's advances, it is not surprising that Patton wrote on the same day that Montgomery's plan was approved, "Books will some day be written on that 'Pause which did not refresh' anyone but the Germans."[30]

Nofi specifically cites the failure of intelligence to locate German units within the area of interest before Operation Market Garden as one of the great mistakes of the operation, and he judges British intelligence's errors as inexcusable. [31] Contrary to the above historical account of intelligence's performance in the planning for Operation Market Garden, ULTRA analysts knew about the above German force deployments almost two weeks before the plans were initiated. This was the type of information that allowed Patton to move confidently, without concern for large, undiscovered units suddenly appearing in his sector. On 5 September ULTRA intercepted the German Army Group B's direction to the "Nine SS Panzer and Ten SS Panzer Division, elements not operating, to be transferred for rest and refit in [the] area of Venloo–Arnhem."[32] The following day, ULTRA messages reiterated the above directive and further ordered, "HQ [Headquarters] Two SS Panzer Corps subordinated [to] Army Group B, to transfer to Eindhoven to rest and refit in cooperation with General of Panzer Troops West and direct rest and refit of 2nd and 116th Panzer Divisions, 9th SS Panzer Division and Heavy Assault Gun Abteilung 217 . . . and 10 SS Panzer Division not operating [is] order[ed] [on the] fourth [of September] to area of Venloo–Arnhem . . . for refit."[33]

Another 5 September ULTRA message from Army Group B to the armed forces commander of the Netherlands specifically made "mention of further withdrawal of 15th Army" and ordered them "to prepare flank protection in the west–east direction on [the] general line [of the] Albert Canal."[34] ULTRA displayed no confusion over the location of these forces.

113

Patton's conscience was clear; he knew these forces were operating in the north. Third Army could proceed against an enemy that had concentrated its forces outside Patton's AOR. What was even more appalling in retrospect was the further disregard of ULTRA information by higher headquarters—information that was emanating from Patton's sector.

Within Patton's zone ULTRA continued to intercept most of the Germans' attempts to rectify their defensive problems. These messages captured the dire nature of the German situation as troops from the south were instructed to construct a "line of defense in [the] sector Chaumont–Chatillon–Sur–Seine as other troops [are] not available and it is a matter of life and death for [the] Army Group to secure the northern flank."[35] The Germans were specifically concerned about the West Wall approaches just beyond Patton's tanks. One ULTRA message received on 5 September highlighted the exact areas of weakness and the ramifications of an Allied attack in this area: "Chief of Staff, Commander-in-Chief West on third [of September]: [The] following are of decisive importance 1) [They need] Exact knowledge of [the] course of the West Wall. 2) Its blocking on the German–Luxembourg and German–French frontier between south of Trier and Merzig. An Allied thrust towards Trier would tear open the existing West Wall before it is made fit for defense . . . All HQ's and units must know it, because it must in all circumstances be defended as a last barrier."[36] The Germans made every effort to fill these gaps in their lines, but there were few resources available. They did not know that Patton's supplies were headed elsewhere, and the Nazis' desperate pleas for support came in the form of the following request: "situation requires [the] speediest employment of engineering blocking forces to prevent surprise [by] forward thrusts by Allied Tanks. Army Group requests employment of Engineer forces, as it has none available."[37] Engineering troops were not the only units needed on the West Wall. Numerous parties requested combat troops, as the following message reveals, "Blumentritt to Jodl . . . [The] gap between Luneville and Belfort cannot be closed at present with own forces until elements of Army Group G have arrived there . . . Commander-in-Chief West again applies for bringing of

114

three infantry divisions in order to close this gap. As Allies consist of armor and motorized infantry divisions, plentifully supplied with tanks. Divisions to be brought up must be adequately supplied with anti-tank weapons. Allocations of panzer brigades specifically desired."[38]

ULTRA, through the CINC west, identified the weak points and also let Patton know how long his window of opportunity would be open, as this 4 September message reveals, "Subordinates concerning [the] protection of the West positions as quoted by Commander-in-Chief West . . . 36th Grenadier Division security garrison line Trier–Saarbrücken, 559th Grenadier Division security garrison line Thionville–Metz, . . . 36th Division not expected to be ready for employment until 15 September but efforts being made to begin transport of first elements by [the] 10th."[39] Even more frustrating for Patton, he not only watched his supplies being sent north but ULTRA also told him the Germans were redirecting additional forces from Third Army's area to Montgomery's sector—reported in the following message: "Hitler order[ed] third [September] 19th Parachute Army subordinated to Army Group B for the defense of [the] Albert Canal from Antwerp to Maastricht. Formation at its disposal to include 3d, 5th, and 6th Parachute Divisions and those elements temporarily engaged in [the] Nancy area."[40] As the evidence continued to build about the hazards associated with an Allied attack in Holland, Patton continued to receive encouraging reports concerning his sector that stated, "[a] second reported gap in [the] front, between Longway and Thionville [and is] only covered by the weak forces of Flak Corps Three, [they are] ready to join in ground fighting. Destruction of [the] remainder of [the] Flak Corps thereby to be expected, so new setting up [of secondary lines is] impossible."[41] Considering the dichotomy between the two axes of attack, it is not surprising Patton considered this episode to be a momentous error in the war.

As with the rest of the drive across France, General Patton knew that the Germans would eventually rectify their problems within their lines if the Allies did not capitalize on the present situation. In order for the Third Army to continue their exploitation, General Eddy implemented one of Patton's unconventional schemes. This time Patton was dealing with hindrances created by his Allies. To overcome these setbacks, he resorted to more desperate measures, as he noted in his diary.

> [SHAEF's Staff] are letting Montgomery overpersuade Ike to go north. It's a terrible mistake, and when it comes out in the after years, it will cause much argument. The British have put it over again. We got no gas because, to suit Monty, the First Army got most of it, and we are also feeding Parisians. When I got back [to headquarters] I found that Eddy had told Gaffey (Third Army Chief of Staff) during my absence that if he pushed on to Commercy, he would arrive with no gas, so Gaffey told him to halt near St. Dizier. I told Gaffey to run till the engines stop and then go on foot . . . In the last war I drained 3/4 of my tanks to keep the other 1/4 going, Eddy can do the same. It is terrible to halt, even at the Meuse. We should cross the Rhine at Worms, and the faster we do it, the less lives and munitions it will take. No one realizes the terrible value of the "unforgiving minute" except me. Some way I will get on yet.[42]

Patton managed to continue to get on, but it was at a much slower pace and required more reliance on ULTRA.

As the above ULTRA intercepts indicated, there was very little threat ahead of Third Army. But due to the fuel situation and XIX TAC being tied up with the Brest operations, Patton was forced to employ weak thrusts to gain bridgeheads. After the Third Army secured the Meuse River crossings, the next target was the Moselle. During this drive the force-enhancing capabilities of ULTRA were again apparent. One example is a high-priority ULTRA message that warned, "intentions [to attack] night of six–seventh according to 82 Corps . . . Support of attack [will be] of 15th PG [Panzer Grenadier] Division in the area of Montmedy–Verdun–Briey–Audun by thrust of a battle-group of 17th SS Panzer Division from Metz bridgehead in direction Conflans."[43] This message made a big impression on Helfers's assistant as he recalled, "a 5 Z message arrived at 0100 o'clock, containing an Army order for an attack at 0300 o'clock by the 15th Pz Gr and 17th SS Pz." The message was taken at once to Colonel Koch who went with the recipient to General Gaffey. Means were devised to warn the division concerned without jeopardizing security. The German attack was planned upon an exposed flank and at a time when the Army was "spread out as thin as the skin on an egg," in General Patton's language. No other form of intelligence could possibly give such advanced warnings."[44] Through these drives Third

Army was able to secure three bridgeheads across the Moselle River near Metz, Nancy, and Toul. But without supplies and with numerous delays, they soon stalled and eventually allowed the Germans the time they needed to build up defensive positions.

As the Operation Market Garden start date of 17 September approached, additional information continued to indicate the dichotomy between the two fronts. Patton's forces idly watched the CINC west initiate desperate measures to rectify the problems with the West Wall, even ordering "all supply troops . . . billeted near the West Wall and all troops of Army, Luftlotte Three, Naval Gruppe West . . . [and] all forces in any way available to be put together in emergency units and to be put in at once for defense of the West Wall."[45] Across from Montgomery was a different story. On 13 September it became apparent that Operation Market Garden might not achieve the surprise it needed. ULTRA intercepted requests for "Air Recce (reconnaissance) for the tenth [September] . . . "to establish whether [the] Allies [were] preparing formations for a thrust to Aachen or against First Para[chute] Army for a thrust towards Arnhem."[46] The next day ULTRA reported "according [to an] unspecified authority [there are] strong indications landing[s] in Netherlands [are] imminent, with [the] employment of large forces."[47] On 15 September (two days before attack), ULTRA produced a long, seven-part message that provided specific details of the upcoming operations that stated "Thirty British Corps [of the] Two British Army between Antwerp and Hasskelt. Bring up further Corps is possible . . . Photo recce tasks indicate probable intention is thrust mainly on Wilhelmina Canal on both sides of Eindhoven into Arnhem. [Bletchley Park provides additional] (Comment: further specification of area incomplete but includes 'west of Nijmegen') To cut off and surround German forces [in] western Netherlands."[48] This information was available to Allied leadership, and they still chose Operation Market Garden as their best route into Germany. Patton's drive in the south was sacrificed to support this attack. Although Patton effectively employed intelligence, it was not enough to have one Army commander using this vital information while others were apparently oblivious.

ULTRA was not the only source providing information about the threatening German forces in the landing zones of Montgomery's forces. The Dutch underground provided secondary confirmation that led officers to confront Montgomery. At the lower levels, Maj Brian Urquhart, intelligence officer at the First Allied Airborne Army, used reports from the Dutch resistance and aerial photos to find the German panzers in a prospective drop zone. Brushed aside, Major Urquhart was judged "hysterical and shortly afterwards was ordered to take a rest and go on leave."[49] At the most senior levels, Gen Kenneth Strong (Eisenhower's chief intelligence officer) and Gen Walter Beddell Smith (SHAEF chief of staff)—both of whom were cleared for ULTRA—were concerned with the evidence of German tanks in the vicinity of Arnhem. General Strong later related in a guarded account (his story was told before the declassification of ULTRA) of this event: "Not long before the air drop on Arnhem, I told Beddell Smith that I had doubts about its success as there were some evidence of German armor, probably new tanks, were within striking distance of Arnhem. General Eisenhower instructed me to go with Beddell Smith to Twenty-first Army Group headquarters in order to explain our fears."[50] These two officers proceeded to Montgomery's headquarters in Brussels; and like Major Urquhart, they had their information dismissed. General Smith recalled of the meeting "I got nowhere, Montgomery simply waved my objection airily aside."[51] The last person to confront Montgomery was Wing Commander Asher Lee, air intelligence officer at the Airborne Army. Lee made a point to read ULTRA, and he "found evidence of armor at Arnhem so conclusive that he used every effort, without success, to bring its significance home to the authorities in England. Lee therefore made his way to Belgium and found that there, too, his warning fell on deaf ears."[52] Montgomery's stubborn refusal to acknowledge ULTRA-based warnings that conflicted with his plans stands in marked contrast to Patton's use of this highly sensitive source.

Operation Market Garden ended with Montgomery categorizing the debacle as "a bridge too far." But this failure reflected much more than that. The bridge to which he referred was the object of the entire operation. The Allies took this route because Montgomery sold senior leadership on the premise that this was the most effective route into the Reich, to the neglect of the southern option. Patton vehemently disagreed with this course of action, and senior ULTRA officer Ralph Bennett's following observation displays Patton's understanding of the situation and the dichotomy between the two schemes of maneuver. "On the basis of ULTRA intelligence alone, then, there was little to choose between the opportunities presented on the lower Rhine and the upper Moselle and Saar, and much to be said in favor of a quick and shattering blow in the latter region (Patton's area of responsibility). Ample information about each was provided with equal accuracy."[53]

Unfortunately, intelligence is not the only factor taken into consideration when making operational decisions within an Allied campaign. Eisenhower had suspicions about the chances for Market Garden, which is probably why he sent General Smith to confront Montgomery; but as Strong notes,

> Many fail to understand the great pressures, both national and international, both hidden and apparent, to which the Supreme Commander was subjected . . . Eisenhower had not only to consider the wider strategy of the campaign, but also to give due weight to the views of those immediately subordinate to him. Montgomery, now a Field-Marshal, was the chief British commander in the field and in close touch with Churchill and the British Chiefs of Staff. Montgomery's views were generally those of the British Government and it was therefore extremely important not to turn down his proposals out of hand.[54]

Eisenhower recalled how Montgomery presented his proposal in this case and stated "he vehemently declared that all he needed was adequate supply in order to go directly into Berlin."[55] Montgomery's insistence on the operation, coupled with strong support from British prime minister Winston S. Churchill and chief of the British Imperial Staff Field Marshal Alan Brooke, may have created a political rationale for the operation. In his memoirs, however, Eisenhower chose to articulate a rationale for the plan that was primarily military: "I instructed him (Montgomery) that what I did in the north was

Antwerp working, and I also wanted a line covering that port. Beyond this I believed it possible that we might, with airborne assistance, seize a bridgehead over the Rhine in the Arnhem region, flanking defenses of the Siegfried Line."[56] Eisenhower may not have believed wholeheartedly Montgomery's plan, but he did approve it. This decision had its consequences, and Eisenhower admitted in 1948: "I am certain that Field Marshal Montgomery, in light of the later events, would agree that this view was a mistaken one."[57]

The Germans also confirmed this mistake. David C. Eisenhower, in *Eisenhower: At War 1943–1945*, highlights the Germans' 1 September 1944 point of view.

> Veterans of the German high command would later agree that bold Allied moves that week might have penetrated the German frontier defenses and ended the war. To his postwar interrogators, Jodl described the difficulties facing the German high command. Under Hitler's ongoing edict to counterattack in Normandy, the military had been severely restricted in preparing for the defense of the Seine, the Somme and the German frontier. "The action of the supreme command upon events in the west was extremely limited," Jodl recalled. "It scarcely had any reserves available and only with reserves can strong influence be exercised . . . for days there was just a general directive, to fight as stubbornly or hold or gain as much ground as possible in order to seal the gaps in the fronts and to gain the necessary time for the West Wall to receive armaments for its defense." Jodl also suggested that determined movement on the Paris–Reims Luxembourg axis towards Frankfurt (Patton's axis), where a single reconnaissance battalion of the Sixth Panzer Army patrolled the Saar Frontier, would have penetrated the toughest sectors of the West Wall.[58]

Von Rundstedt echoed the above comments, noting "that at this time the Allies could have broken through the West Wall whenever they wished . . . But to our great surprise the operations of the Allies came to a full stop in front of the West Wall: supply difficulties were presumably at the root of this."[59] Supplies were the problem, and on 25 September (the last day of Operation Market Garden), Third Army received the following order: "The acute supply situation confronting us has caused the Supreme Commander to direct until further orders, the Third Army with its supporting troops, and those elements of the Ninth Army placed in the line, will assume the defensive . . . This change in attitude on our part must be completely concealed from the enemy."[60] This order may have been kept secret from the Germans, but its ramifications became very clear to the enemy because it was the first week of November before Third Army was to make another major offensive. Patton's letter to his wife on 25 September best encapsulated the situation when he wrote "it was not the Germans who have stopped us, but higher strategy."[61]

During this campaign, Patton had to overcome many hindrances that were beyond his control. One by one, his force enhancers disappeared via competing interests. Airpower was diffused by two different tasks. The XIX TAC was sent 500 miles to the rear to deal with the strong defenses at Brest, and his airlift capabilities were denied due to humanitarian efforts in Paris and Montgomery's efforts in the north. His rapid drives were not focused on land or headlines but on time. Patton knew if the enemy was granted any respite, Third Army would pay for these delays in lives and time. The denial of supplies left Patton with very few force-enhancing capabilities, and ULTRA could only carry the Third Army so far. Patton was an avid consumer of ULTRA, and the higher headquarters' disregard for this information must have been particularly frustrating. But as he found out, it was not enough for him to understand the battle space, his superiors must be equally informed or they might be tempted to initiate any offensive against an enemy that was apparently kaput.

The Allies obviously chose a poor path as their main effort into the Third Reich; and the extreme delays caused by Operation Market Garden continued to prove Patton's theory about delays correct, as General Harkins reflected. "We had to hold up for a while, while they put up the effort north on Montgomery . . . By the time we started again, they filled in the Siegfried Line in and around Metz, and we had a he---of-a-time getting through there."[62] As Patton predicted, the decisions made during this phase of World War II caused much argument. In May 1945 the assistant chief of staff for air intelligence contributed to the debate. His report was very critical on the diversion of XIX TAC to hit fortresses in the extreme west; and he called Brest, St. Malo, and Isle de Cezembre (island of St. Malo) "three battered monuments to the uneconomical use of air power."[63] This same report forwarded the counterfactual proposition that stated, "It is tempting to speculate on what would have happened if the entire lift of our strategic bomber force had been temporarily committed to the hauling of freight for Third Army."[64] Eventually, the Third Army did prevail after a long delay. But more important for future commanders are Patton's two observations associated with this campaign and the costs of failing to apply the right resources against the correct targets.

> He [Eisenhower] kept talking about the future great battle of Germany, while we assured him that the Germans have nothing left to fight with if we push on right now. If we wait, there *will* be a future great battle of Germany.[65]

> Montsec has a huge monument to our dead (World War I). I could not help but think that our delay in pushing forward would probably result, after due course of time, in the erection of many other such monuments for men who, had we gone faster, would not have died.[66]

All decisions have their consequences. Some would argue the consequences associated with the diversion of supplies and airpower and the disregard of intelligence in this campaign resulted in all of the losses associated with not ending the war earlier.

Notes

1. Great Britain Public Record Office, "ULTRA: Main Series of Signals Conveying Intelligence," Bletchley Park, 1944, reels 36 and 37, XL 6450 and 6881. Copy located in Auburn University Library, Auburn, Ala.

2. Seymour Freidin, Werner Kreipe, and William Richardson, eds., *The Fatal Decisions* (New York: W. Sloan Associates, 1956), 235.

3. Martin Blumenson, *Breakout and Pursuit* (Washington, D.C.: Office of the Chief of Military History, Department of the Army, 1961), 657–58.

4. Martin Blumenson, *The Patton Papers*, vol. 2, *1940–1945* (Boston: Houghton Mifflin, 1974), 527.

5. Freidin, Kreipe, and Richardson, 232.

6. Blumenson, *Breakout and Pursuit*, 667–68.

7. Freidin, Kreipe, and Richardson, 235.

8. Great Britain Public Record Office, reel 39, XL 8994.

9. Blumenson, *The Patton Papers*, 530.

10. George S. Patton Jr., Paul D. Harkins, and Beatrice A. Patton, *War as I Knew It* (Boston: Houghton Mifflin, 1947), 120.

11. Blumenson, *Breakout and Pursuit*, 663–64.

12. Patton, Harkins, and Patton, 119–20.

13. Great Britain Public Record Office, reel 38, XL 7872 and 7979.

14. Blumenson, *The Patton Papers*, 532.

15. O. P. Weyland, Report 168.7104-1—"Weyland Diary—XIX TAC" (Albert F. Simpson Historical Research Center: Weyland Collection, 18 May 1945), diary for 2 September 1944, no time given.

16. XIX TAC Staff, Report 168.7104-90—"XIX TAC—Tactical Air Operations in Europe" (Albert F. Simpson Historical Research Center: Weyland Collection, May 1945), 1.

17. XIX TAC Staff, XIX TAC—"Tactical Air Operations in Europe," 48.

18. Great Britain Public Record Office, reel 34, XL 4931.

19. Ibid., reel 35, XL 5655.

20. Willis Thornton, Report 533.4501-9—"Effects of Air Attacks on the Fortress of St. Malo" (Albert F. Simpson Historical Research Center: Aerospace Studies Institute, 22 August 1944), 1.

21. XIX TAC Staff, "XIX TAC—Tactical Air Operations in Europe," 48–49.

22. Great Britain Public Record Office, reel 40, XL 9138.

23. Ibid., XL 9598.

24. Blumenson, *The Patton Papers*, 543.

25. XIX TAC Staff, "XIX TAC—Tactical Air Operations in Europe," 50.

26. Oscar W. Koch and Robert G. Hays, *G-2: Intelligence for Patton* (Philadelphia: Whitmore Publishing, 1971), 66.

27. Blumenson, *Breakout and Pursuit*, 687.

28. Thomas Parrish, *The American Codebreakers: The US Role in ULTRA* (Chelsea, Mich.: Scarborough Press, 1991), 254.

29. Albert A. Nofi, *The War against Hitler: Military Strategy in the West* (New York: Hippocrene Books, 1982), 157–58.

30. Blumenson, *The Patton Papers*, 546.

31. Nofi, 172–73.

32. Great Britain Public Record Office, reel 40, XL 9188.

33. Ibid., XL 9245.

34. Ibid., XL 9162.

35. Ibid., reel 39, XL 8815.

36. Ibid., reel 40, XL 9174.

37. Ibid., reel 39, XL 8987.

38. Ibid., reel 40, XL 9104.

39. Ibid., XL 9100.

40. Ibid., XL 9247.

41. Ibid., XL 9143.

42. Blumenson, *The Patton Papers*, 531.

43. Great Britain Public Record Office, reel 40, XL 9310.

44. Warrack Wallace, SRH-108—"Report on Assignment with the Third United States Army 15 August–18 September 1944" (National Archives: Record Group 457, 21 May 1945), 4.

45. Great Britain Public Record Office, reel 40, XL 9597.

46. Ibid., reel 41, HP 9.

47. Ibid., HP 175.

48. Ibid., HP 242.

49. Ronald Lewin, *ULTRA Goes to War: The First Account of World War II's Greatest Secret Based on Official Documents* (London: Hutchinson Co., 1978), 349–50.

50. Kenneth Strong, *Intelligence at the Top: The Recollections of an Intelligence Officer* (Garden City, N.Y.: Doubleday, 1969), 202.

51. Lewin, 350.

52. Ibid., 351.

53. Ralph Francis Bennett, *ULTRA in the West: The Normandy Campaign, 1944–45* (New York: Scribner, 1980), 135–36.

54. Strong, 203.

55. Dwight D. Eisenhower, *Crusade in Europe* (Garden City, N.Y.: Doubleday, 1948), 305.

56. Ibid., 307.

57. Ibid., 305.

58. David C. Eisenhower, *Eisenhower: At War 1943–1945* (New York: Random House, 1986), 436.

59. Freidin, Kreipe, and Richardson, 235.

60. Third US Army, "After Action Report, 1 Aug 44–9 May 45," vol. 1, Third US Army September Operations, Regensburg, Germany, 1945, 84. Copy located in Auburn University Library, Auburn, Ala.

61. Blumenson, *The Patton Papers*, 556.

62. James Hasdorff, Report K239.0512-522—"Interview with General Paul D. Harkins" (Air Force Historical Research Center: Corona Harvest Collection, 23 February 1972), 10–11.

63. Office of the Assistant Chief of Air Staff for Intelligence, Report 168.7104-92—"IMPACT—US Tactical Air Power in Europe" (Albert F. Simpson Historical Research Center: Weyland Collection, May 1945), 30.

64. Ibid., 31.

65. Blumenson, *The Patton Papers*, 537.

66. Patton, Harkins, and Patton, 124.

Chapter 7

Conclusions and Implications

Does ULTRA, of World War II, have significant lessons for us today? I think it does. Cracking enemy secret codes and other signal devices and improvisations do help, but the only sure path to victory is to have a united, determined people with able and decisive leadership, predominant resources and military power.

—Gen Ira C. Eaker

In December 1974 General Eaker analyzed the Allies' employment of ULTRA in World War II. Eaker's survey commended generals such as Patton for their quality of generalship and, in contrast, said: "Montgomery and Mark Clark stand out as brave but often timid souls whose failure to exploit ULTRA in a timely and decisive fashion cost the Allies dearly."[1] But as the above epigraph indicates, ULTRA was only one factor on the path to victory; and if all the other factors are neglected in war, they cost a nation dearly. All the major commanders within the European theater had access to ULTRA, and their units were largely outfitted with similar equipment. But General Patton often produced results that far exceeded those of the other commanders during this campaign. During his operations Patton understood the fluid conditions that existed in France in 1944. He crafted a plan that exploited this situation with a unique and complementary employment of ULTRA, airpower, and ground maneuver. These force elements allowed him to continue his drives east as his AOR grew exponentially. Third Army and XIX TAC's drive across France demonstrated that Patton's trinity had a complementary momentum of its own. More importantly, it also exhibited the adverse effects associated with denying any one of these aspects to a commander. General Patton was one of the most successful and feared commanders of the European theater, and his drive across France had numerous lessons for the future. As

General Eaker pointed out, the failure of other commanders to employ these force enhancers correctly cost the Allies dearly.[2] Therefore, it is imperative that we learn the significant lessons from Patton's 1944 campaign. These insights will be developed from historical conclusions on the areas of intelligence, ground maneuver, airpower, and leadership.

Intelligence

General Patton's drive across France clearly demonstrated that accurate, timely information concerning enemy dispositions and intentions can be invaluable to campaign planning and—more significantly—to the adjustment of the campaign as it moves toward its objective. The Mortain counteroffensive illustrated that ULTRA could shape the planning of battle. Through preconceived ULTRA plans, air and ground power became a cool, poised, and fully briefed reception committee that rapidly destroyed the German forces in a set-piece battle under conditions that were changed to favor the Allies.[3] Patton also applied ULTRA to make rapid adjustments to exploit the sparse defenses between the Seine River and the German border. Due to competing Allied efforts, Patton was forced to employ weak thrusts to capture bridgeheads; and ULTRA ensured that the applicable assets would be employed to counter any German threats as Third Army was "spread out as thin as the skin on an egg."[4]

Overall, ULTRA clearly influenced Patton's operations and allowed him to adopt economy-of-force measures to contend with his expanding AOR. Patton's statement that ULTRA saved him "the service of two divisions" illustrated in objective terms ULTRA's force-enhancing capacity.[5] For XIX TAC, ULTRA reduced the search area south of the Loire; identified vulnerable airfields; aided in the interdiction of supplies, troops, and equipment; and provided accurate bomb damage assessments and flak warnings. But perfect intelligence such as ULTRA will not guarantee overwhelming success, as demonstrated by the striking contrast between the operational achievements of Patton's Third Army and other Allied commands.

ULTRA employment in France in 1944 demonstrated the significant influence of the human element on the use of operational intelligence. General Patton handpicked Colonel Koch to be his G-2, and Koch cited his close relationship with his commander as one of the key elements of a successful intelligence operation.

> Command support—the support of his commander, evidenced primarily by mutual confidence engendered by and nurtured through respect. He must be confident that the results of his efforts will be respected by his commander, both in terms of interest and attitude and in the degree of utilization of the end product so painstakingly produced. The commander on the other hand must be confident that his intelligence chief's work merits such respect. If either confidence fails, command support is nonexistent. With command support, G-2 will tackle any job. Without it, he performs a useless task, merely going through a series of staff exercises. In that case, both he and the commander are losers.[6]

Colonel Koch had command support, and the issue of confidence in G-2 personnel had significant implications for the Allies' ULTRA program. Before the Normandy campaign began, a civilian lawyer decided "that lawyers as a class are better fitted for intelligence work."[7] Although these men were extremely intelligent (one later becoming a Supreme Court justice), in the eyes of some Regular Army officers they were a "bunch of civilian lawyer flunkies."[8] Such an appearance could undermine a commander's confidence in his intelligence team. This was not an issue within Patton's headquarters because Major Helfers (the only Regular Army ULTRA officer) and Major Grove (a World War I pilot) had instant credibility and therefore had command support almost immediately. Helfers and Grove did not perform worthless staff exercises. Patton utilized the end product, and one of Third Army's ULTRA assistants lamented, "It's a pity that the thousands who contribute in one mechanical way or another to the finished product cannot share in the drama attending its final use in the field."[9] Unlike Montgomery's staff at Market Garden, Koch, Helfers, and Grove had Patton's support and confidence, which was one of the key elements of Patton's employment of intelligence during this campaign.

Effective intelligence also demands effective distribution. Perhaps the greatest strength of Patton's ULTRA program was his ability to push relevant information down to subordinate commands. Patton's employment of ULTRA destroyed many of the previous assumptions associated with this high-level source of information. As one ULTRA officer noted, "The service (ULTRA) often is said to be primarily of strategic value and only useful tactically in a static situation. Perhaps its prime value is strategic, but Patton's use of ULTRA in his historic drive across France is a fitting thesis for a tactical epic."[10] This tactical epic demonstrated the rapid and flexible employment of information that influenced all levels of Patton's operations. The campaign was also marked by numerous instances of Patton testing the ULTRA guidelines that governed the employment of this source. Although Helfers had some nervous experiences during this campaign, Koch's big picture often produced acceptable cover stories for ULTRA's employment. And it was obviously successful because the Germans did not discover the compromise of the Enigma machine until 1974 when Group Capt Winterbotham published *The Ultra Secret*.

Ground Maneuver

Throughout this campaign Patton's forces demonstrated that when an attacker grants a reprieve to a retreating force, the pause will eventually cost more in lives and equipment than the more ambitious alternative. During this drive Patton argued, "It is terrible to halt . . . We should cross the Rhine in the vicinity of Worms, and the faster we do it, the less lives and munitions it will take. No one realizes the terrible value of the unforgiving minute except me."[11] The validity of this proposition is clearly demonstrated when one compares the rate of advance and losses after the Third Army's halt at Falaise and on the banks of the Seine. The Germans used the time granted by the Allies' halt orders to prepare and consolidate the remnants of their once defeated forces to construct defenses that significantly hindered Patton's operations. The greatest example of this concept is the delay associated with the diversion of resources to support Montgomery's Market Garden. This pause allowed the Germans to prepare the West Wall, which would postpone Patton's entry into Germany by almost six months at a significant cost of lives and equipment. The failure to exploit the conditions opposite Patton's front has often been cited by former German leadership as one of the most significant Allied errors of the war as reflected in the following statement:

> Veterans of the German high command would later agree that bold Allied moves that week might have penetrated the German frontier defenses and ended the war . . . [Generaloberst Alfred] Jodl also suggested that determined movement on the Paris–Reims Luxembourg axis towards Frankfurt (Patton's axis), where a single reconnaissance battalion of the Sixth Panzer Army patrolled the Saar Frontier, would have penetrated the toughest sectors of the West Wall [Patton's sector of operations].[12]

General Zimmerman echoed these veterans of the high command with the following passage: "It was Rundstedt's conviction that at this time [early September 1944] the Allies could have broken through the West Wall whenever they wished . . . But to our great surprise the operations of the Allies came to a full stop in front of the West Wall: supply difficulties were presumably at the root of this."[13]

This campaign also demonstrated how ground maneuver could aid Patton's other force enhancers. Patton's ground scheme of maneuver facilitated ULTRA because it forced the Germans to depend on the wireless Enigma machine. Whether the Germans were retreating to Germany or back to their fortresses, these actions generated volumes of ULTRA traffic that led Bletchley Park representatives to recall the increase in intercepts to "unprecedented levels."[14] The ground scheme of maneuver also assisted the air campaign by capturing German airfields. These new fields allowed airpower to be rapidly applied on the battlefield with increased loiter times and better sortie generation rates. Patton's rapid advance also secured areas away from the unfavorable weather conditions of the Cherbourg Peninsula.

Airpower

One of the most impressive accomplishments of this campaign was the destructive firepower generated by the airground team of XIX TAC and Third Army. Patton highlighted their complementary nature when he noted, "Armor can move fast enough to prevent the enemy having time to deploy off the roads, and so long as he stays on the roads, the fighter-bomber is one of the most deadly opponents."[15] John C. Slessor argued that airpower should be "concentrated where its influence was most likely to be decisive at the time," a criterion that perfectly described the cooperation between Third Army and XIX TAC.[16] With air superiority in favor of the Allies, Weyland employed aircraft as the point for armor columns and provided constant, on-call CAS. These activities, complemented by XIX TAC's interdiction operations, caused Patton to write Gen Henry H. "Hap" Arnold, chief of the Army Air Corps, stating that "for about 250 miles I have seen the calling cards of the fighter-bombers."[17]

XIX TAC performed several functions that aided Patton's advance. XIX TAC served as flank guard for almost 500 miles of territory, and it also secured several rear areas. These actions allowed Patton to redirect troops ordinarily dedicated to the above roles to become spearheads for Third Army's advancing columns. XIX TAC's bombing ensured that enemy ground forces were denied respite on any area of the battlefield. Therefore, they were not able to "hardwire" communications, which once again induced German dependence on the wireless Enigma machine, thus generating exploitable information. Air reconnaissance missions also provided quick cover stories for the operational employment of ULTRA. Finally, although limited in overall tonnage, airpower was employed to keep Patton's rapid drives pushing forward through the use of IX Troop Carrier Command. This organization moved supplies more rapidly than could the ground-based Red Ball Express. Eventually, this service and some of XIX TAC's efforts were diverted to other, less profitable objectives, which leads to a final observation.

Commanders must know the limitations of their systems, learn from the previous battles, and employ the lessons learned to future scenarios. The diversion of the XIX TAC to Brest was a mistake. The POWs from St. Malo provided ample evidence that the fighter-bomber was ineffective against the Brittany forts, and ULTRA reports reconfirmed this fact. XIX TAC would add little to the 31 artillery battalions employed against this objective, which should have been merely contained. In contrast, the XIX TAC had exhibited outstanding results against troops in travel mode; and during this period the Rhone Valley and Loire River areas provided fertile conditions for effective fighter-bomber sorties. This denial of a force enhancer provided an additional example of the recurring frustration that occurred when Patton was denied these assets during his campaign.

Leadership

This study sheds a new light on Patton's leadership during the campaign in France, particularly regarding his calculation of risk and the steps he took to minimize it. Patton's generalship was a key to Third Army's successful integration of intelligence, the ground scheme of maneuver, and airpower. When Patton was afforded all of the elements of his force-enhancing trinity, Third Army produced unprecedented gains and overwhelming victories—such as the battle of Mortain. His employment of these elements allowed him to choose which battles he would fight and which he would avoid. Those he chose to fight allowed him to make rapid gains with relatively few losses. In contrast, when either air or ground operations were hindered by higher headquarters' orders, the other two elements attempted to offset the deficiencies; but the results never rose to the same high level of accomplishments. These mutually supporting enhancers eventually had a momentum of their own that rolled the Germans back to within 50 miles of their borders. But as this study has demonstrated, when leaders fail to exploit the conditions associated with a weakened enemy or neglect to employ their assets effectively, the cost in war is paid in precious lives and materiel. Considering this great price, it is imperative that we learn the lessons from the past that this campaign has for the future.

Implications for the Future

This campaign provides counsel to future leaders who incorrectly believe that information dominance or perfect information will solve all of the problems on the battlefield. ULTRA may have been a very reliable source of information; but without credibility on the part of the data analysts, it was not always well integrated into the commanders' operational concepts. It is not surprising that after World War II one report suggested that "if Special Security Officers [ULTRA officers] are recruited from the ranks of those who have had intelligence experience, then they will need less training, and then they will be better Special Security Officers."[18] This study calls into question the practice of placing cross-trainees into critical intelligence positions because such officers could be as ineffective as bad British troops or civilian lawyer flunkies, which would negate the efforts of the numerous individuals who painstakingly produced the intelligence product. But as Colonel Koch pointed out in regard to General Patton, this is only half the equation. Commanders themselves must have a useful appreciation for intelligence in order to apply this information effectively in battle. Patton had two tours as an intelligence officer. Assigning future air commanders to intelligence billets may not be practical in today's US Air Force; but absent such a policy, the present state of intelligence instruction at our professional military education schools must be improved. A greater understanding of intelligence sources and methods may be the first step towards Koch's command support, which in his words will ensure that in future battles, the "G-2 will tackle any job."[19]

Effective dissemination is also vital. One of the factors that made Patton so successful was his employment of high-level intelligence in low-level situations. Future intelligence leaders must remember that people at the lowest levels do not care if the information comes from an Enigma machine or a POW report. When General Bayerlein was asked to "judge American intelligence," he stated "[the] intelligence service must have worked well, for generally tactical targets were recognized swiftly and correctly."[20] He and the rest of the Germans did not even suspect that the Allies' intelligence successes were due to a compromise of the Enigma machine. This lack of perception suggests that future "intelligence gain/loss studies" should not focus on the worst-case scenario because within a robust intelligence program, there are always cover stories available.

The Third Army–XIX TAC cooperation also demonstrates the importance of air-ground operations, notwithstanding the airpower successes in Kosovo and Bosnia. Some analysts are extrapolating from the events in the Balkans a vision of single-service operations as the future of warfare. This is a mistake. These air-only extrapolations could destroy the air-ground synergy that was so prominent in Patton's campaigns and that could well be required in future campaigns. Furthermore, the use of "kill boxes" during Desert Storm to strike targets well beyond friendly lines was very successful; but the Patton–Weyland form of air-ground cooperation will require much more intimate teamwork. And Patton's version of the World War II evolution of air-ground cooperation may have lessons for today: "We have seen the attempts of air and ground to work together for years but it was only on the 1st of August [1944] that it really worked. First, air was subservient to the ground forces. That was wrong. Then air and ground were set as things apart and that was wrong, for it was quite evident that we were not getting along."[21] Whether the Army and the Air Force are getting along is not the point. In World War II Patton had the luxury of improving his use of airpower through an evolutionary process. In future battles we may not be afforded the luxury of time in which to develop the most effective form of air-ground cooperation. Sensor-to-shooter initiatives have the possibility of paying handsome returns in a rapid integrated air-ground campaign, but the techniques to perfect these initiatives will require extensive joint practice in peacetime. The Air Force and Army must ensure that all information systems are compatible and—more importantly—that these two services practice on a large scale with these new information dominance initiatives. There are numerous possibilities to increase this training—from joint Red Flags and National Training Center ventures to remote simulations incorporated into one large exercise. These exercises should resolve some of the problems that took Patton years in World War II to correct. They should also ensure the most effective application of information, airpower, and ground forces in future operations.

At the end of Patton's campaign across France, General Spaatz traveled to Nancy, France, to congratulate the XIX TAC and Third Army for their outstanding August and September campaign. Spaatz gave a speech saying "I'd like to congratulate you for your work in France. What you've seen is the greatest example of air-ground cooperation that has ever been or ever will be." Patton responded, "General Spaatz you are a liar. What we are going to do will make the crossing of France look like chicken sh--," and then he immediately sat down.[22] Unfortunately, due to a diversion in resources, Patton was only able to replicate his 1944 movements for brief periods beyond the borders of France.

The crossing of France was quite remarkable. Harkins and Weyland both went on to become full generals; and they both agreed with Spaatz's opinion, claiming that they had not seen an air-ground effort as successful as the XIX TAC and Third Army's. Therefore, the first portion of Spaatz's comments are clearly true; but it is up to us and our leaders to ensure that Spaatz is proven a liar in future conflicts that require extensive intelligence and air-ground coordination. If the Air Force and the Army both learn the proper lessons from this campaign concerning how best to integrate intelligence, ground maneuver, and airpower, the best will, indeed, be yet to come.

Notes

1. Ira C. Eaker, Microfilm 23342—Personal Collection of I. C. Eaker—"ULTRA Goes to War" (Air Force Historical Research Center: Eaker Collection, 29 December 1974), 2.

2. Ibid.

3. Ronald Lewin, *ULTRA Goes to War: The First Account of World War II's Greatest Secret Based on Official Documents* (London: Hutchinson Co., 1978), 338.

4. Warrack Wallace, SRH-108—"Report on Assignment with the Third United States Army 15 August–18 September 1944" (National Archives: Record Group 457, 21 May 1945), 4.

5. Melvin C. Helfers, video tape interview at The Citadel (Charleston, S.C.: The Citadel Archives, 9 October 1984).

6. Oscar W. Koch and Robert G. Hays, *G-2: Intelligence for Patton* (Philadelphia: Whitmore Publishing Co., 1971), 165.

7. Alfred McCormack, SRH-185—"War Experiences of Alfred McCormack" (National Archives: Record Group 457, 31 July 1947), 4.

8. Melvin C. Helfers, Personal Papers—"My Personal Experience with High Level Intelligence" (Charleston, S.C.: The Citadel Archives: November 1974), 10.

9. Wallace, 4.

10. Ibid., 3–4.

11. Martin Blumenson, *The Patton Papers,* vol. 2, *1940–1945* (Boston: Houghton Mifflin, 1974), 531.

12. David C. Eisenhower, *Eisenhower: At War 1943–1945* (New York: Random House, 1986), 436.

13. Seymour Freidin, Werner Kreipe, and William Richardson, eds., *The Fatal Decisions* (New York: W. Sloan Associates, 1956), 235.

14. Ralph Francis Bennett, *ULTRA in the West: The Normandy Campaign, 1944–45* (New York: Scribner, 1980), 119–20.

15. George S. Patton Jr., "General Patton's Own Story," *Saturday Evening Post,* 1 November 1947, 16.

16. John C. Slessor, *Air Power and Armies* (London: Oxford University Press, 1936), 79.

17. Carlo D'Este, *Patton: A Genius for War* (New York: HarperCollins Publishers, 1995), 637.

18. SRH-107, "Problems of the SSO System in World War II" (National Archives: Record Group 457, 17 September 1945), 35.

19. Koch and Hays, 165.

20. Willis Thornton, Report 168.7104-95—"Interrogation of General Fritz Bayerlein" (Albert F. Simpson Historical Research Center: Weyland Collection, 29 May 1945), appendix 1-7.

21. O. P. Weyland, Report 168.7104-101—"Talks by General Patton and General Weyland at Press Conference" (Albert F. Simpson Historical Research Center: Weyland Collection, 16 December 1944), 3.

22. Frederick Vosburg, XIX TAC senior intelligence officer, telephone interview with the author, 24 March 2000.

Bibliography

Allen, Robert S. *Lucky Forward.* New York: Vanguard Press, 1947.

Ayer, Fred, Jr. *Before the Colors Fade.* Boston: Houghton Mifflin, 1964.

Bennett, Ralph Francis. *ULTRA in the West: The Normandy Campaign, 1944–45.* New York: Scribner, 1980.

Blumenson, Martin. *The Battle of the Generals: The Untold Story of the Falaise Pocket.* New York: Morrow, 1993.

———. *Breakout and Pursuit.* Washington, D.C.: Office of the Chief of Military History, Department of the Army, 1961.

———. *Patton, The Man behind the Legend, 1885–1945.* New York: Morrow, 1985.

———. *The Patton Papers.* Vol. 2, *1940–1945.* Boston: Houghton Mifflin, 1974.

Boyd, Carl. *Hitler's Japanese Confidant: General Oshima Hiroshi and Magic Intelligence, 1941–1945.* Lawrence: University Press of Kansas, 1993.

Bradley, Omar N. *A Soldier's Story.* New York: Henry Holt Co., 1951.

Church, George C. SRH-023—"Reports by US Army ULTRA Representatives in the European Theater of Operations." National Archives: Record Group 457, 28 May 1945.

D'Este, Carlo. *Patton: A Genius for War.* New York: HarperCollins Publishers, 1995.

Eaker, Ira C. Microfilm 23342—Personal Collection of I. C. Eaker—"ULTRA Goes to War." Air Force Historical Research Center: Eaker Collection, 29 December 1974.

Eisenhower, David C. *Eisenhower: At War 1943–1945.* New York: Random House, 1986.

Eisenhower, Dwight D. *Crusade in Europe.* Garden City, N.Y.: Doubleday, 1948.

Fellers, James D. SRH-023—"Reports by US Army ULTRA Representatives in the European Theater of Operations." National Archives: Record Group 457, 30 May 1945.

Field Manual (FM) 100-20. *Command and Employment of Air Power,* 21 July 1943.

Forty, George. *Patton's Third Army at War.* London: Arms and Armour Press, 1990.

Freidin, Seymour, Werner Kreipe, and William Richardson, eds. *The Fatal Decisions.* New York: W. Sloan Associates, 1956.

French, Jules K. Report 168.7104-38—"Report of Activities of Liaison Officer with German Marsch Gruppe Sud." Air Force Historical Research Center: Weyland Collection, 20 September 1944.

Great Britain Public Record Office. "ULTRA: Main Series of Signals Conveying Intelligence." Bletchley Park, 1944. Reels 33–41. Copies located in Auburn University Library, Auburn, Ala.

Griggs, John C. SRH-023—"Reports by US Army ULTRA Representatives in the European Theater of Operations." National Archives: Record Group 457, 17 May 1945.

Grove, Harry M. SRH-023—"Reports by US Army ULTRA Representatives in the European Theater of Operations." National Archives: Record Group 457, 30 May 1945.

Hasdorff, James. Report K239.0512-522—"Interview with Gen Paul D. Harkins." Air Force Historical Research Center: Corona Harvest Collection, 23 February 1972.

Helfers, Melvin C. Personal Papers—"My Personal Experience with High Level Intelligence." Charleston, S.C.: The Citadel Archives, November 1974.

————. Video tape interviews at The Citadel. Charleston, S.C.: The Citadel Archives, 2, 9, and 16 October 1984.

Hinsley, F. H. British Intelligence in the Second World War: Its Influence on Strategy and Operations. New York: Cambridge University Press, 1979.

Hitchcock, Edward. "The Hut Six Story." Foreign Intelligence Literary Scene, June 1982.

Irving, David. Hitler's War. New York: Viking Press, 1977.

Jepson, Gerry B. Report 533.4501-9—"Assessments of Air Attacks as Determined from Prisoners of War." Albert F. Simpson Historical Research Center: Aerospace Studies Institute, 18 August 1944.

Koch, Oscar W., and Robert G. Hays. G-2: Intelligence for Patton. Philadelphia: Whitmore Publishing Co., 1971.

Kozaczuk, Wladyslaw. Enigma: How the German Machine Cipher Was Broken, and How It Was Read by the Allies in World War Two. Frederick, Md.: University Publications of America, 1984.

Kuter, Laurence S. "God---mit Georgie." Air Force Magazine, February 1973.

Lewin, Ronald. Montgomery as Military Commander. Conshohocken, Penn.: Combined Publishing, 1998.

———. *ULTRA Goes to War: The First Account of World War II's Greatest Secret Based on Official Documents.* London: Hutchinson Co., 1978.

Marshall, George C. SRH-026—"Marshall Letter to Eisenhower on the Use of ULTRA Intelligence." National Archives: Record Group 457, 15 March 1944.

McCormack, Alfred. SRH-185—"War Experiences of Alfred McCormack." National Archives: Record Group 457, 31 June 1947.

National Security Agency. Report 170.601-5—"Magic Reports for the Attention of the President." Albert F. Simpson Historical Research Center: Special Collections, 1943–1944.

IX Troop Carrier Command Staff. Report K110.7006-2—"Special Project File." Albert F. Simpson Historical Research Center: Research Studies Institute, 30 November 1944.

XIX TAC Staff. Report 168.7104-64—"Twelve Thousand Fighter-Bomber Sorties." Albert F. Simpson Historical Research Center: Weyland Collection, 30 September 1944.

———. Report 168.7104-81—"Planes over Patton." Albert F. Simpson Historical Research Center: Weyland Collection, 30 October 1944.

———. Report 168.7104-82—"XIX Tactical Air Command Daily Intelligence Summary." Albert F. Simpson Historical Research Center: Weyland Collection, September 1944.

———. Report 168.7104-85—"Operation Plan: Air Support of Third Army's Drive to the East." Albert F. Simpson Historical Research Center: Weyland Collection, 23 August 1944.

———. Report 168.7104-90—"XIX TAC—Tactical Air Operations in Europe." Albert F. Simpson Historical Research Center: Weyland Collection, May 1945.

———. Report 168.7104-101—"Fly, Seek, and Destroy." Albert F. Simpson Historical Research Center: Weyland Collection, 13 December 1944.

Nofi, Albert A. *The War against Hitler: Military Strategy in the West.* New York: Hippocrene Books, 1982.

Nye, Roger H. *The Patton Mind: The Professional Development of an Extraordinary Leader.* Garden City Park, N.Y.: Avery Publishing, 1993.

Office of the Assistant Chief of Air Staff for Intelligence. Report 168.7104-92—"IMPACT—US Tactical Air Power in Europe." Albert F. Simpson Historical Research Center: Weyland Collection, May 1945.

Parrish, Thomas. *The American Codebreakers: The US Role in ULTRA.* Chelsea, Mich.: Scarborough Press, 1991.

Patton, George S., Jr. "General Patton's Own Story." *Saturday Evening Post,* 1 November 1947.

Patton, George S., Jr., Paul D. Harkins, and Beatrice A. Patton. *War as I Knew It.* Boston: Houghton Mifflin, 1947.

Pierce, Mark L., et al. *Hammond Atlas of the World Second Edition.* Maplewood, N.J.: Hammond, 1999.

Province, Charles M. *Patton's Third Army: A Daily Combat Diary.* New York: Hippocrene Books, 1992.

Rosengarten, Adolph G. SRH-023—"Reports by US Army ULTRA Representatives in the European Theater of Operations." National Archives: Record Group 457, 21 May 1945.

Slessor, John C. *Airpower and Armies.* London: Oxford University Press, 1936.

SRH-023, "Synthesis of Experiences in the Use of ULTRA Intelligence by US Army Field Command in the European Theater of Operations." National Archives: Record Group 457, 27 May 1945.

SRH-107, "Problems of the SSO System in World War II." National Archives: Record Group 457, 17 September 1945, 35.

SRH-113, "ULTRA History of the US Strategic Air Force Europe versus German Air Forces." National Archives: Record Group 457, May 1945.

Spires, David N. "Air Power for Patton's Army: The XIX Tactical Air Command in the Second World War," draft paper, June 1994, Boulder, Colo.

Stephenson, Ralph. Report K239.0512-813—"Interview with Gen O. P. Weyland." Air Force Historical Research Center: Weyland Collection, 19 November 1974.

———. Report K239.0512-838—"Interview with Lt Gen Elwood R. Quesada—ULTRA Section." Air Force Historical Research Center: Quesada Collection, 13 May 1975.

Strong, Sir Kenneth. *Intelligence at the Top: The Recollections of an Intelligence Officer.* Garden City, N.Y.: Doubleday, 1969.

Third US Army. "After Action Report, 1 Aug 44–9 May 45." Vol. 1, Annex 1: Twelfth US Army Group Directives, Regensburg, Germany, 1945. Copy located in Auburn University Library, Auburn, Ala.

———. "After Action Report, 1 Aug 44–9 May 45." Vol. 1, Annex 4: Third US Army Outline Plan, Regensburg, Germany, 1945. Copy located in Auburn University Library, Auburn, Ala.

———. "After Action Report, 1 Aug 44–9 May 45." Vol. 1, Annex N, Third US Army Directives, Regensburg, Germany, 1945. Copy located in Auburn University Library, Auburn, Ala.

———. "After Action Report, 1 Aug 44–9 May 45." Vol. 1, Third US Army August Operations, Regensburg, Germany, 1945. Copy located in Auburn University Library, Auburn, Ala.

Thornton, Willis. Report 168.7104-95—"Interrogation of General Fritz Bayerlein." Albert F. Simpson Historical Research Center: Weyland Collection, 29 May 1945.

———. Report 533.4501-9—"Effects of Air Attacks on the Fortress of St. Malo." Albert F. Simpson Historical Research Center: Aerospace Studies Institute.

Vosburg, Frederick. XIX TAC senior intelligence officer, telephone interview with the author, 24 March 2000.

Wallace, Brenton G. Patton and His Third Army. Washington: Military Service Publishing Co., 1946.

Wallace, Warrack. SRH-108—"Report on Assignment with the Third United States Army, 15 August–18 September 1944." National Archives: Record Group 457, 21 May 1945.

Weigley, Russell F. Eisenhower's Lieutenants: The Campaign of France and Germany, 1944–1945. Bloomington, Ind.: Indiana University Press, 1981.

Weyland, O. P. Report 168.7104-1—"Weyland Diary—XIX TAC." Albert F. Simpson Historical Research Center: Weyland Collection, 18 May 1945.

———. Report 168.7104-95—"Weyland's Interrogation of von Rundstedt at Bad Kissingen." Albert F. Simpson Historical Research Center: Weyland Collection, 2 July 1945.

———. Report 168.7104-101—"Talks by General Patton and General Weyland at Press Conference." Albert F. Simpson Historical Research Center: Weyland Collection, 9 December 1944.

———. Report 168.7104-101—"Talks by General Patton and General Weyland at Press Conference." Albert F. Simpson Historical Research Center: Weyland Collection, 16 December 1944.

————. Report 168.7104-114—"XIX Tactical Air Command Pictorial History." Albert F. Simpson Historical Research Center: Weyland Collection, 29 May 1986.

Wilson, Wasson J., and Henry F. Fitzmaurice. Report 248.401-19—lecture,"Command and Employment of Airpower." Air Force Historical Research Center, 10 January 1945 (really 1944 by internal evidence).

Winterbotham, F. W. *The Ultra Secret.* New York: Harper & Row, 1974.